A SOURCEBOOK FOR ENGAGING WITH CIVIL SOCIETY ORGANIZATIONS IN ASIAN DEVELOPMENT BANK OPERATIONS

DECEMBER 2021

ADB

ASIAN DEVELOPMENT BANK

ISBN 978-92-9269-244-5 (print); 978-92-9269-245-2 (electronic); 978-92-9269-246-9 (ebook)
Publication Stock No. SGP210506-2
DOI: http://dx.doi.org/10.22617/SGP210506-2

Note:
In this publication, "$" refers to United States dollars.

On the cover: ADB believes in civil society engagement. Different civil society organizations in Bangladesh, India, Maldives, the People's Republic of China, and Viet Nam, along with other countries in the region, are ADB's partners in implementing meaningful and sustainable development projects across Asia and the Pacific (photos by ADB).

Cover design by Jasper Lauzon

Contents

Tables, Figures, and Boxes

Foreword

The Asian Development Bank (ADB) is committed to strengthening its engagement with civil society organizations (CSOs). CSOs bring unique strengths and specialized knowledge of their communities and constituencies and are an invaluable ally in the fight against poverty. CSOs make meaningful contributions across ADB's seven Strategy 2030 operational priorities, sector, and thematic areas, and can provide important inputs to boost the impact of ADB-financed operations. Working with CSOs helps ADB and its developing member countries (DMCs) deliver improved development outcomes.

A Sourcebook for Engaging with Civil Society Organizations in Asian Development Bank Operations is a valuable resource for DMC officials and ADB staff to assist ADB achieve its vision for a prosperous, inclusive, resilient, and sustainable Asia and the Pacific. This guide outlines the entry points for CSO engagement in policy and strategy development and review, including country programming, and throughout the project cycle. It also provides guidance on important issues such as procurement, partnerships, and the important roles that CSOs can play in accountability, transparency, and good governance.

To strengthen CSO engagement in ADB-financed operations, DMC officials and staff will benefit from this publication. The 2021 Sourcebook, an update of ADB's 2009 Sourcebook, contains information, tips, and guidance on the why, what, when, and how of CSO engagement. The sourcebook is a compilation of all aspects of CSO engagement in ADB-financed operations, and, for the first time, presents the guidance in one place.

I encourage DMC officials and ADB staff engaged with CSOs to refer to the sourcebook to enhance CSO activity already planned or underway. They may also utilize it to explore innovative ways of engaging with CSOs for future projects. Those less experienced in working with CSOs can read the sourcebook to identify opportunities for how CSOs may contribute, and for seeking new ways in which ADB, DMCs, and CSOs can collaborate to achieve common objectives.

I am pleased to present ADB's 2021 *A Sourcebook for Engaging with Civil Society Organizations in Asian Development Bank Operations*.

Bruno Carrasco
Director General
Sustainable Development and Climate Change Department

Acknowledgments

This sourcebook was prepared by staff and consultants of the NGO and Civil Society Center (NGOC), Asian Development Bank (ADB). NGOC consultant Emma Walters prepared the sourcebook under the guidance of Elaine Thomas (former NGOC senior staff specialist). Other NGOC staff contributed to the publication, including Oliver Chapman, Ma. Catherine P. Malilay, Christopher Morris, Roselle Rasay, and Jose Luis Syquia. Other ADB staff contributed sections, including Steven J. Goldfinch, Beatrice Yulo Gomez, Francesco Tornieri, and ADB consultants Jaime Antonio, Jr., Brenda Batistiana, Elizabeth De Benedetti, Marino Deocariza, and Marlene C. Fuentes. Peer reviewers from Plan International Asia and Pacific and the National Commission for Women and Children, Bhutan reviewed the publication. This publication draws substantially from the 2009 ADB *CSO Sourcebook* assembled by Bart W. Édes, then head, NGOC. Many ADB staff members provided inputs to the publication. Special thanks to those who commented on early drafts of this publication. Monina M. Gamboa edited the publication, and Nonie Villanueva was responsible for layout and design.

Introduction

Strategy 2030, the long-term corporate strategy of Asian Development Bank (ADB), outlines ADB's vision for a prosperous, inclusive, resilient, and sustainable Asia and the Pacific.[1] Under Strategy 2030, ADB has committed to strengthening its engagement with civil society organizations (CSOs). ADB engages with a range of CSOs to strengthen the effectiveness, quality, and sustainability of the activities it supports.

In 2021, ADB updated its 2003 Operations Manual Section E4 on *Promotion of Engagement with Civil Society Organizations*.[2] Also in 2021, ADB published the Staff Instruction on *Promotion of Engagement with Civil Society Organizations*,[3] which provides guidance on the policy and compliance requirements for CSO engagement in ADB-financed operations.[4]

This sourcebook complements these publications. It provides guidance, advice, templates, and tips on maximizing the benefits of engaging with CSOs to assist ADB staff and developing member country (DMC) officials work with CSOs in designing, implementing, and monitoring ADB-financed operations. This is an update of ADB's 2009 *CSO Sourcebook: A Staff Guide to Cooperation with Civil Society Organizations*.[5]

Who is this sourcebook for? This sourcebook is designed for DMC officials, ADB staff, ADB consultants, and other consultants involved in ADB-financed operations.[6] It provides this audience with detailed advice and guidance on how to operationalize CSO engagement across policy development and review, country programming, and throughout the project cycle.

How to use this sourcebook. ADB staff and DMC officials should refer to the Contents and determine what specific information on CSO engagement they are seeking, and refer to the section.

The main sections of the sourcebook, with the key information each section contains and the target audience for each section, are as follows:

1. **Context, Definitions, and Overview**: This section covers the context of CSO engagement, including the Sustainable Development Goals and the policy basis for ADB's engagement with CSOs. It provides ADB's definition of CSOs, in the context of other development partners' definitions of CSOs. It introduces the four approaches to participation and how these are defined within the context of

---

[1]   ADB. 2018. Strategy 2030: Achieving a Prosperous, Inclusive, Resilient, and Sustainable Asia and the Pacific. Manila.
[2]   ADB. 2021. Promotion of Engagement with Civil Society Organizations. *Operations Manual*. OM E4. Manila.
[3]   ADB. 2021. *Staff Instruction on Promotion of Engagement with Civil Society Organizations*. Manila.
[4]   Where reference is made to "ADB-financed operations" throughout this publication, this phrase is taken to include wholly ADB-financed operations plus ADB-assisted and ADB-administered operations.
[5]   ADB. 2009. *CSO Sourcebook: A Staff Guide to Cooperation with Civil Society Organizations*. Manila.
[6]   Where reference is made to "ADB staff" and "DMC officials" throughout this publication, this is understood to include the consultants who support these groups.

ADB-financed operations. This section is relevant to all users of this sourcebook, as it provides the key and necessary concepts for CSO engagement.

2. **Policy and Operations:** This section covers roles for CSOs in ADB-financed operations. It provides guidance for preparing or reviewing a policy with CSO engagement, engaging CSOs during country programming, engaging with CSOs in the project cycle, and tracking CSO engagement in ADB operations. This section is particularly relevant for ADB staff and DMC officials engaging with CSOs at the policy and strategy level, particularly during country partnership strategy preparation and review, and for those working on ADB-financed projects, across all phases of the project cycle.

3. **Consultations with Civil Society Organizations**: This section provides useful tips and guidance for consultations with CSOs, which may be used during policy development and review, in country programming, or at any point in the ADB project cycle. This section is relevant to those ADB staff and DMC officials that have responsibility for consultations with CSOs.

4. **Due Diligence, Procurement, and Partnerships**: This section covers how to identify suitable CSOs and how to assess the capacity of CSOs. It also covers engagement of CSOs in procurement, including how to publicize procurement opportunities to CSOs. It covers nonconsulting services and engaging CSOs as consulting firms. It addresses (i) framework agreements with CSOs, (ii) output-based contracts and terms of reference, (iii) contracting CSOs, (iv) special considerations for procurement in fragile and conflict-affected situations, and (v) how to engage with small CSOs. This section also addresses community participation in procurement and showcases case studies where innovative approaches to procurement have been successfully applied. This section concludes with a discussion of ADB's partnerships with CSOs. The text on identifying and assessing the capacity of CSOs is relevant to all readers. The part on procurement is relevant for ADB staff preparing technical assistance, plus ADB staff and DMC officials preparing or implementing loans or grants. The text on partnerships is relevant primarily to ADB staff, as DMCs will have their own defined processes for developing partnerships with CSOs.

5. **Other Considerations for Civil Society Organization Engagement**: This section covers additional ways to engage with CSOs in fragile and conflict-affected situations (FCAS); disaster and emergency situations; at the resident mission and representative office level; in pilot activities; in nonsovereign operations; and under activities supporting good governance, anticorruption, ADB's Accountability Mechanism, and access to information. It also covers CSO engagement via country safeguard systems, activities designed to localize the Sustainable Development Goals, as a conduit to citizen engagement, CSO engagement at ADB annual meetings, and secondments to ADB from CSOs. It discusses the paramount importance of the relationship with DMC governments, and offers guidance on engaging with CSO advocacy organizations. It concludes with a series of frequently asked questions on CSO engagement in ADB-financed operations. This section contains useful information for all readers.

6. **Responsibilities for Civil Society Organization Engagement Within ADB**: Responsibility for CSO engagement within ADB-financed operations is covered in this section, and is of interest to all readers.

The sourcebook provides examples and templates to facilitate the engagement of CSOs in ADB operations. Many of these examples and templates are linked and are available on ADB's NGO and Civil Society Center's community site on SharePoint, for ADB staff. ADB intends to use this website to create an ever-growing repository of tools, resources, and templates to assist ADB to work with CSOs throughout ADB operations.

DMC officials and ADB staff are encouraged to read this guide in conjunction with ADB's 2012 guide to participation, *Strengthening Participation for Development Results: An Asian Development Bank Guide to Participation*. Additionally, the sourcebook refers to ADB guidance and policy material—readers should consult the source material to determine the authoritative policy and compliance requirements.[7]

The sourcebook complements existing resources ADB has produced on increasing CSO engagement in ADB-financed activities, including e-learning, case studies, guidance materials, and templates. Visit the ADB and Civil Society webpage for more information. ADB has launched an online learning suite, Deepening Civil Society Engagement in ADB-financed Operations, through ADB's eLearn. Three e-learning modules are available: one each for ADB staff, DMC officials, and staff of CSOs.

In summary, the sourcebook is designed as a valuable and complementary tool for ADB staff and DMC officials to use for exploring opportunities to increase engagement with CSOs on ADB-financed operations, for a more prosperous, inclusive, resilient, and sustainable Asia and the Pacific.

---

[7] Cited source guidance and policy material may be updated from time to time. Readers should consult the source material for the latest and authoritative versions: in case of a discrepancy between this publication and the cited guidance and policy material as updated from time to time, the latter will hold.

Abbreviations

ADB	Asian Development Bank
AIP	Access to Information Policy
CBO	community-based organization
CCA	climate change adaptation
CMS	consultant management system
COVID-19	coronavirus disease 2019
CPS	country partnership strategy
CQS	consultant qualification selection
CRF	corporate results framework
CSO	civil society organization
DMC	developing member country
DMF	design and monitoring framework
DOC	Department of Communications
DRR	disaster risk reduction
EOI	expression of interest
FBS	fixed-budget selection
FCAS	fragile and conflict-affected situations
FRA	fragility and resilience assessment
GAP	gender action plan
GBV	gender-based violence
GESI	gender equality and social inclusion
ICT	information and communication technology
IPSA	initial poverty and social analysis
JFPR	Japan Fund for Prosperous and Resilient Asia and the Pacific
KPA	knowledge partnership agreement
NGO	nongovernment organization
NGOC	NGO and Civil Society Center
NSO	nonsovereign operation
OAI	Office of Anticorruption and Integrity
OGP	Open Government Partnership
OP	operational priority
OPP	operational plan for priority
OPD	organization of people with disabilities
PAM	project administration manual
PAP	project-affected people

PCR	project completion report
PMU	project management unit
PPFD	Procurement, Portfolio, and Financial Management Department
PSA	poverty and social analysis
QBS	quality-based selection
QCBS	quality- and cost-based selection
RRP	report and recommendation of the President
SDAP	social development action plan
SDCC	Sustainable Development and Climate Change Department
SDG	Sustainable Development Goal
SEAH	sexual exploitation, abuse, and harassment
SIDS	small island developing states
SPRSS	summary poverty reduction and social strategy
TA	technical assistance
TOR	terms of reference
WASH	water, sanitation, and hygiene
YfA	Youth for Asia

1

Context, Definitions, and Overview

The Asian Development Bank's Commitment to Civil Society Organization Engagement

The Asian Development Bank (ADB) is committed to exploring opportunities to increase its engagement with civil society organizations (CSOs). As part of this commitment, in 2021, ADB updated its 2003 Operations Manual Section E4 on *Promotion of Engagement with Civil Society Organizations.*[1] Also in 2021, ADB published the Staff Instruction on *Promotion of Engagement with Civil Society Organizations.*[2] These documents provide clear guidance for both ADB and developing member country (DMC) staff working on the policy and compliance requirements for CSO engagement in ADB-financed operations. This sourcebook complements these documents and provides ADB and DMC staff with advice, tips, examples, technical direction, and templates on **why**, **what**, **when**, and **how** to engage with CSOs on ADB-financed operations.

ADB's *Strategy 2030: Achieving a Prosperous, Inclusive, Resilient, and Sustainable Asia and the Pacific*[3] sets the course for ADB's strategic direction and includes its ambitions for engaging with CSOs. Para. 108 of Strategy 2030 sets the scene for ADB's engagement with CSOs (Figure 1).

This ambition to explore opportunities for increasing its engagement with CSOs is outlined in ADB's updated Operations Manual Section E4 *Promotion of Engagement with Civil Society Organizations* (footnote 1) and partly reproduced in Box 1.

---

[1] ADB. 2021. Promotion of Engagement with Civil Society Organizations. *Operations Manual.* OM E4. Manila.
[2] ADB. 2021. *Staff Instruction on Promotion of Engagement with Civil Society Organizations.* Manila.
[3] ADB. 2018. *Strategy 2030: Achieving a Prosperous, Inclusive, Resilient, and Sustainable Asia and the Pacific.* Manila.

Figure 1: Strategy 2030—ADB's Ambition to Strengthen Engagement with Civil Society Organizations

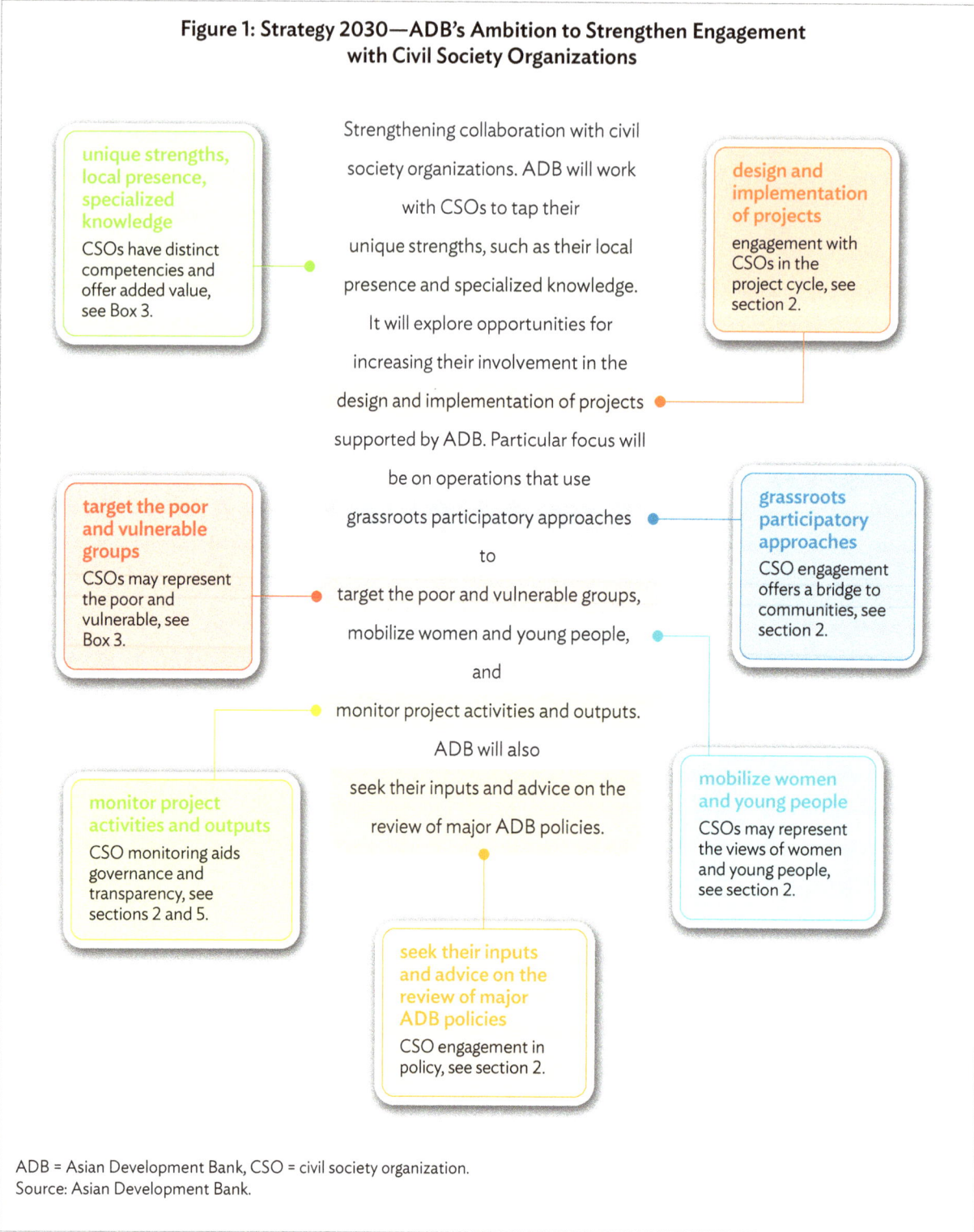

unique strengths, local presence, specialized knowledge
CSOs have distinct competencies and offer added value, see Box 3.

target the poor and vulnerable groups
CSOs may represent the poor and vulnerable, see Box 3.

monitor project activities and outputs
CSO monitoring aids governance and transparency, see sections 2 and 5.

Strengthening collaboration with civil society organizations. ADB will work with CSOs to tap their unique strengths, such as their local presence and specialized knowledge. It will explore opportunities for increasing their involvement in the design and implementation of projects supported by ADB. Particular focus will be on operations that use grassroots participatory approaches to target the poor and vulnerable groups, mobilize women and young people, and monitor project activities and outputs. ADB will also seek their inputs and advice on the review of major ADB policies.

design and implementation of projects
engagement with CSOs in the project cycle, see section 2.

grassroots participatory approaches
CSO engagement offers a bridge to communities, see section 2.

mobilize women and young people
CSOs may represent the views of women and young people, see section 2.

seek their inputs and advice on the review of major ADB policies
CSO engagement in policy, see section 2.

ADB = Asian Development Bank, CSO = civil society organization.
Source: Asian Development Bank.

BOX 1

ADB's long-term corporate strategy, Strategy 2030, outlines ADB's vision for a prosperous, inclusive, resilient, and sustainable Asia and the Pacific. Under Strategy 2030, ADB has committed to strengthening its engagement with CSOs.

ADB pursues an expanded program of engagement with CSOs, where appropriate, in its member countries, in consultation with the government, with a view to strengthen the effectiveness, sustainability, and quality of the development services ADB provides. The objective of ADB's engagement with CSOs, where appropriate, is to tap the unique strengths of CSOs, such as their local presence and specialized knowledge, in order to explore opportunities for increasing their involvement in ADB operations and to seek their inputs and advice on major ADB policies. ADB explores this engagement such that the development efforts ADB supports will more effectively address the issues and priorities reflected in ADB's development agenda.

ADB = Asian Development Bank, CSO = civil society organization.
Source: ADB. 2021. Promotion of Engagement with Civil Society Organizations. *Operations Manual.* OM E4. Manila.

The global context and the Sustainable Development Goals

ADB's engagement with CSOs exists within the global context of engagement with CSOs in development, and their increasingly influential role in setting and directing the development agenda. Following the Paris Declaration on Aid Effectiveness in 2005,[4] the global civil society movement campaigned for civil society to have a clear role in the global aid effectiveness debate. CSOs were recognized internationally as important and influential in development, and as development actors in their own right, at the Third High-Level Forum of Aid Effectiveness at Accra, Ghana, in 2008.[5]

At the Fourth High Level Forum on Aid Effectiveness in Busan, Republic of Korea in 2011,[6] civil society was recognized as a full and equal actor. Busan created the mandate to progress the aid effectiveness debate through the Global Partnership for Effective Development Co-operation,[7] which acknowledges civil society's role and concerns about aid effectiveness. The Global Partnership also provided civil society a permanent seat on the Global Partnership Secretariat.

ADB's work to strengthen collaboration with CSOs aligns with the focus of the Sustainable Development Goals (SDGs). To support achievement of the goals, ADB aligns its strategy and operations to the SDGs. The seven operational priorities of ADB's Strategy 2030 all support the SDGs, and ADB's corporate results framework is aligned with the SDGs. The SDGs recognize the importance of partnership between government, civil society, private sector, and donors. Specifically, SDG Goal 17 commits countries to revitalize global partnerships for sustainable development and encourages effective civil society cooperation.

---

[4]   OECD. Paris Declaration on Aid Effectiveness, Paris, 28 February–2 March 2005.
[5]   OECD. Third High Level Forum on Aid Effectiveness.
[6]   OECD. Fourth High Level Forum on Aid Effectiveness.
[7]   Global Partnership for Effective Development Co-operation. Welcome to the Global Partnership.

Specifically relating to CSO engagement, SDG Goal 16 promotes more inclusive development which can be achieved through responsive, inclusive, participatory, and representative decision-making at all levels (Box 2).

BOX 2

Goal 16
Promote just, peaceful and inclusive societies

Targets include:
Ensure responsive, inclusive, participatory, and representative decision-making at all levels.

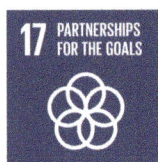

Goal 17
Revitalize the global partnership for sustainable development

"In light of the consequences of the global COVID-19 pandemic, we have seen that strengthening multilateralism and global partnerships are more important than ever if we are to solve the world's problems. The Sustainable Development Goals remain the framework for building back better. We need everyone to come together—governments, civil society, scientists, academia and the private sector."

Targets include:
Encourage and promote effective public, public–private, and civil society partnerships, building on the experience and resourcing strategies of partnerships.

COVID-19 = coronavirus disease.
Source: United Nations. Sustainable Development Goals.

CSO competencies and the added value they may bring to ADB-financed operations

Underpinning its commitment to strengthening CSO engagement, ADB recognizes that CSOs bring special competencies and add value to its operations; and engaging with CSOs can strengthen development effectiveness and improve development outcomes.

Some of the competencies and added value CSOs may bring to ADB operations are outlined in Box 3.

BOX 3

Expertise in local development issues. CSOs generally have an in-depth understanding of local development issues and firsthand experience of social and environmental issues and their presence in difficult-to-reach communities makes them a good partner. They can provide valuable insights into project design and strengthen implementation strategies. In fragile and conflict-affected situations, they may often be more effective than commercial firms (as they often have existing presence in communities, understanding of the issues, and are able to respond swiftly) and be able to support government when capacity is stretched. Professional associations and think tanks, along with other CSOs, can often provide specialized technical expertise in their respective areas.

Linking ADB, government agencies, the private sector, and communities. Where links are weak, CSOs can build bridges between people in communities and government agencies, development institutions, donors, and business organizations. CSOs such as international and national NGOs, labor unions, and CSO (including community-based organization [CBO]) umbrella organizations can connect their constituents with national government agencies and large business organizations. CSOs operating locally can connect with local government agencies, local business organizations, and other CSOs at national and regional levels. Larger or more experienced CSOs can provide management and support to increase the effectiveness of local or smaller CSOs.

Mobilizing communities and awareness raising. CSOs have a great deal of experience organizing and mobilizing communities to achieve development outcomes. Many CSOs are formed to champion the interests of the poor and are willing to work in remote areas. Many CSOs have had outstanding success in community mobilization and awareness raising. Some international CSOs are well-informed about global best practices, while local CSOs may understand local culture better.

Representing vulnerable groups. CSOs are well placed to represent vulnerable groups such as ethnic minorities, indigenous groups, informal sector workers, hard-to-reach remote populations, migrants, internally displaced and/or conflict-affected people, persons with disabilities, unsupported youth, returning refugees, HIV/AIDS-affected individuals and households, older persons, and women. CSOs can provide expertise in participatory planning and consultations, providing voice and agency to communities, and poor and vulnerable groups.

Innovating. Many local CSOs are small organizations with flat management structures and can easily respond to changing and emergency situations. They are often willing and able to experiment with new ideas and innovative approaches to emerging development challenges affecting the communities they work with. They can also co-create solutions and innovations with other partners. CSOs can test small-scale, community-level initiatives before scaling-up to city-level scale among ADB projects.

Providing services. CSOs can be service providers at different levels. They can fill gaps when government services are not available. Governments sometimes contract CSOs to implement their programs. CSOs can be service providers at the regional and national levels, for example, to manage water supplies, microcredit groups, and other community services. They can also provide support to implement ADB's safeguard policy and can support meaningful community safeguarding of impacts of ADB projects, such as facilitating grievance redress mechanisms.

continued on next page

Box 3 continued

Assessment, monitoring, and evaluation. CSOs can do participatory assessments during a project design phase, and independent monitoring and evaluation during project implementation and on completion. CSO monitors are important in promoting good governance, social accountability, and transparency. Some CSOs and research institutes specialize in rapid participatory research techniques, and have experience implementing participatory assessments and monitoring and evaluation.

Independent watchdogs and advocates. CSOs can play an important role as independent watchdogs and advocates. They may be able to focus the attention of governments and the private sector on issues which may be ignored, suppressed, or otherwise inadequately managed. They have a role in maintaining and defending civil society and civic space, and in improving governance and accountability. This is particularly important where there are disadvantaged groups, environmental concerns, or where local people or the media may not have an independent voice.

ADB = Asian Development Bank, CSO = civil society organization, NGO = nongovernment organization.
Sources: ADB. 2012. *Strengthening Participation for Development Results: An Asian Development Bank Guide to Participation.* Manila; and ADB. 2015. *How Does ADB Engage Civil Society Organizations in its Operations? Findings of an Exploratory Inquiry in South Asia.* Manila.

The following demonstrates some varied roles CSOs may play to assist ADB in achieving better development outcomes. Box 4 focuses on CSO roles and contributions in vaccination programs, but CSOs can partner with governments in further aspects of the overall coronavirus disease (COVID-19) response.

BOX 4

COVAX,[a] the global initiative to provide innovative and equitable access to COVID-19 vaccines for people in all corners of the world regardless of their wealth, is working closely with CSOs. Around the world, CSOs are creating awareness, participation, and demand for immunization at the community level, particularly in hard-to-reach communities.

At national and local levels, and in fragile and conflict-affected areas, CSOs and governments build on their experience working together on immunization and other health services in the following areas:
(i)   community outreach to educate, dispel misinformation, and influence behaviors;
(ii) assessing and mitigating the main reasons for vaccine hesitancy;
(iii) identifying those who are vulnerable to missing vaccinations due to demand barriers (e.g., mobility, language, identity, remoteness, and others), and take remedial measures;
(iv) monitoring compliance with the vaccine allocation criteria, helping close gaps in vaccine service delivery, and providing vaccinations when authorized;

continued on next page

Box 4 continued

(v) monitoring integrity in procurement and distribution of vaccine-related goods and services; and

(vi) working with audit and anticorruption agencies using participatory methods.

An ADB TA, Mitigating the Impact of COVID-19 through Community-Led Interventions, is seeking to help countries in Asia and the Pacific engage with CSOs to mitigate the impact of COVID-19 through work in local communities.[b] This program can also be used to increase coverage and equity of COVID-19 vaccination programs across the region. More information on this TA is in Boxes 13 and 20.

ADB = Asian Development Bank, COVAX = COVID-19 Vaccines Global Access, COVID-19 = coronavirus disease, CSO = civil society organization, TA = technical assistance.
[a] World Health Organization. COVAX.
[b] ADB. Mitigating the Impact of COVID-19 through Community-Led Interventions.
Source: C. Morris and V. Bhargava. 2021. Civil society organizations can be a powerful tool in getting people vaccinated. Asian Development Blog. 3 March.

Definition and Types of Civil Society Organizations

ADB defines "civil society organization" in Box 5.

BOX 5

The term "civil society organization" refers generically to organizations (i) not based in government, and (ii) not created to earn profit. ADB defines CSOs as nonprofit organizations independent from the government, which operate around common interests. They vary in size, interests, and function, and include nongovernment organizations (NGOs), youth groups, community-based organizations, independent academic and research institutes, professional associations, foundations, faith-based organizations, people's organizations, and labor unions. CSOs represent interests of their members or others.

ADB = Asian Development Bank, CSO = civil society organization.
Source: ADB. 2021. Promotion of Engagement with Civil Society Organizations. *Operations Manual*. OM E4. Manila.

CSOs included within this definition encompass women's organizations, organizations of people with disabilities (OPDs), identity organizations, indigenous people's groups and environmental groups, program and project-based CSOs, political foundations, social economy and social entrepreneurship organizations, youth development organizations, people's or citizen organizations or initiatives, other groups (sporting clubs, parent-teacher associations, art appreciation societies, volunteers, and others), independent mass organizations, social movements, and coalitions or networks of CSOs and umbrella organizations.

A word on terminology: CSOs and NGOs

Since the adoption of the original Operations Manual Section E4 in 2003, the term "nongovernment organization" (NGO) has evolved. Development partners now use the term "civil society organization," because it considers a broader range of actors, which includes, but is not limited to NGOs. The terms "nongovernment organization" and "NGO" are sometimes used interchangeably with "civil society organization" and "CSO," but NGOs should be properly understood as a subset of CSOs involved in development cooperation. Constituency-based organizations, such as trade unions or professional associations, for example, often do not self-identify as NGOs, but rather as CSOs.[8]

Most development partners take a broader view of the definition of "civil society organization" to expand from the standard understanding of NGOs (e.g., nonprofit organizations, independent of government, that provide or advocate the provision of services relating to economic and social development, human rights, public welfare, or emergency relief). The expanded definition of CSOs includes organizations not traditionally understood within the narrower NGO definition, such as trade unions, business associations, professional associations or federations, and foundations. This sourcebook uses "civil society organization" as the broader sector that incorporates NGOs (Figure 2). Accordingly, when referring to the broader civil society sector, it uses the terms "CSO" and "CSOs" rather than "NGO" and "NGOs." The term "NGO" is used throughout this sourcebook only in reference to organizations that explicitly identify themselves as an NGO. Examples of these organizations that self-identify as NGOs include the International NGO Forum on Indonesian Development, NGO Little Bees International (Japan), and the Dalit Welfare Organization (Nepal).

Figure 2: Nongovernment Organizations are One Sector among Civil Society Organizations

NGO = nongovernment organization.
Source: L.C. Thomas et al. 2019. Participation Tools for the Pacific – Part 1: Engaging Pacific Civil Society Organizations. Development Asia. Manila. Adapted from CIVICUS.

---

8   UNDP. 2013. *Working With Civil Society in Foreign Aid: Possibilities for South-South Cooperation?* Beijing.

A simple way to determine whether an organization is a CSO is to ask the following three questions:

(i) **Is it part of government?** Remember that intergovernment organizations such as United Nations Development Programme, UNICEF, and World Health Organization are part of government.

(ii) **Is it for-profit?** Remember that business associations, chambers of commerce, and others are not-for-profit, even though they represent the for-profit or market sector. Also remember that some CSOs conduct social enterprises and divert revenue surplus to the activities of the CSO—in this case, these are still regarded as not-for-profit.

(iii) **Is it part of the family unit?**

If the answer to each of these about an organization is "no," it is most likely a CSO.

BOX 6

OECD Development Assistance Committee

CSOs can be defined to include all nonmarket and nonstate organizations outside of the family in which people organize themselves to pursue shared interests in the public domain. They cover a wide range of organizations that include membership-based CSOs, cause-based CSOs, and service-oriented CSOs. Examples include community-based organizations and village associations, environmental groups, women's rights groups, farmers' associations, faith-based organizations, labor unions, cooperatives, professional associations, chambers of commerce, independent research institutes, and the not-for-profit media.[a]

World Bank

The wide array of nongovernmental and not-for-profit organizations that have a presence in public life, express the interests and values of their members and others, based on ethical, cultural, political, scientific, religious, or philanthropic considerations.[b]

European Bank for Reconstruction and Development

For the EBRD's purposes, civil society includes NGOs, policy and research think tanks, social movements, labor unions, community-based organizations, women's groups, business development organizations, and other socioeconomic and labor-market actors, including individual activists.[c]

CIVICUS

CIVICUS' definition of civil society is broad and covers nongovernmental organizations, activists, civil society coalitions and networks, protest and social movements, voluntary bodies, campaigning organizations, charities, faith-based groups, trade unions, and philanthropic foundations.[d]

continued on next page

Box 6 continued

African Development Bank
The myriad of civic organizations in civil society includes, but are not limited to, NGOs, people's and professional organizations, trade unions, cooperatives, consumer and human rights groups, women's associations, youth clubs, independent radio, television, print and electronic media, neighborhood or community-based coalitions, religious groups, academic and research institutions, grassroots movements, and organizations of indigenous peoples.[e]

CSO = civil society organization, EBRD = European Bank for Reconstruction and Development, NGO = nongovernment organization, OECD = Organisation for Economic Co-operation and Development.
[a] OECD. 2009. *Civil Society and Aid Effectiveness: Findings, Recommendations and Good Practice*. Paris: OECD Publishing.
[b] The World Bank. Civil Society.
[c] European Bank for Reconstruction and Development. Civil Society Engagement Overview.
[d] CIVICUS. Who we are.
[e] African Development Bank Group. 2015. *Framework for Enhanced Engagement with Civil Society Organizations*. Abidjan.

Types of civil society organizations

Some CSOs are membership-based, and some are not. Some CSOs are member organizations and represent those members' interests (i.e., nurses' associations, water users' groups, international member-based CSOs [such as Greenpeace, Amnesty International, and AIESEC], older women's networks, youth organizations, and others), and some CSOs represent the interests of nonmembers (i.e., councils of social services, Marie Stopes International).

Community-based organizations. Community-based organizations (CBOs) are generally organized to directly address the immediate concerns of their members. CBOs typically represent their members' interests. A key characteristic of CBOs is that they can mobilize communities by expressing demands, organizing, and implementing participatory processes, accessing external development services, and sharing benefits among members. They have a wide range of functions that encompass activities relating to economic, social, religious, and even recreational issues. Some CBOs will be formal legal entities and/or registered with the government or a peak CSO, while others may be unregistered associations or collectives. Examples of CBOs include neighborhood associations, youth groups, women's groups, tenant associations, community development organizations, water-user groups, and credit associations.

Development civil society organizations. These organizations address social and humanitarian issues relating to development, individual and community welfare and well-being, and poverty. They may also address environmental and natural resource protection, management, and improvement.

Organizations of people with disabilities. OPDs are a specialist type of CSO. OPDs are representative organizations or groups of persons with disabilities, where persons with disabilities constitute a majority of the overall staff, board, and volunteers at all levels of the organization. It includes organizations of relatives of persons with disability (only those representing children with disabilities, people with intellectual disabilities, and/or the Deafblind) where a primary aim of these organizations is empowerment and the growth of self-advocacy of persons with disabilities. OPDs have an understanding of disability in accordance with the social model, which notes that barriers are caused by society, rather than by a person's disability.[9]

Faith-based organizations. These are religious-based groups organized around a place of religious worship or congregation, a specialized religious institution, or a registered or unregistered institution with a religious character or mission. CSOs with a religious foundation may also fall under this category. Examples include Buddhism for Development, Islamic Relief Worldwide, Muhammadiyah, Caritas, and World Vision.

Foundations. Foundations are also CSOs if they are not-for-profit and nongovernment. An example is The Asia Foundation: The Asia Foundation is a nonprofit international development organization committed to improving lives across a dynamic and developing Asia.[10] These are often philanthropic or charitable organizations set up by individuals or institutions as a legal entity (a corporation or trust) that support causes consistent with the goals of the foundation. They may also be organized as charitable entities that receive donations for the purpose of financing specific activities that are often of a cultural or socially beneficial nature. Other examples include the Ayala Foundation (The Philippines), Aga Khan Foundation (Switzerland), Sir Ratan Tata Trust (India), Amata Foundation (Thailand), Jeffrey Cheah Foundation (Malaysia), Goh Foundation (Singapore), the Bill and Melinda Gates Foundation (United States), and the Ford Foundation (United States).

International nongovernment organizations. Perhaps the simplest definition of an international NGO (INGO) is that provided in Resolution 288 (X) of the United Nations Economic and Social Council (27 February 1950): "any international organization that is not founded by an international treaty." Typically (but not exclusively) headquartered in a developed country, international NGOs include ActionAid, Cooperative for Assistance and Relief Everywhere International, Mercy Corps, BRAC, HelpAge Asia, Plan International, Save the Children, Transparency International, WWF, Conservation International, and World Vision.

Labor unions. Labor unions are formally organized associations of workers who have united to advance their collective views regarding wages, hours of work, and working conditions. Labor unions are often organized on an industry- or occupation-specific basis. They frequently associate themselves with umbrella federations, congresses, and networks such as the Indonesian Trade Union Congress, the India National Trade Union Congress, Public Services International, and the International Trade Union Confederation.

Nongovernment organizations. ADB has historically used the term "NGO" almost synonymously with "CSO" to include all not-for-profit organizations that are independent of the state. Nowadays, the term "NGO" refers more narrowly to professional, intermediary, and nonprofit organizations that provide or advocate the provision of services relating to economic and social development, human rights, public welfare, or emergency relief. Examples of NGOs that identify as such are given in section 1.

People's organizations. These are grassroots volunteer organizations that advance the economic and social well-being of their members. While in some countries the term "people's organizations" is used interchangeably with "CBO" or it is used as a general term for membership organizations of poor, excluded, and vulnerable people, the term more likely refers to organizations that address concerns relating to a particular sector, such as artisanal fisherfolk, rather than a particular geographic location. Other examples of people's organizations include those formed by farmers, women's groups, local laborers, informal workers, or indigenous peoples.

---

9   Adapted from Disability Rights Fund. What is a DPO?
10 The Asia Foundation.

Private sector representative organizations. CSOs can also be formed to represent the interests of the private sector. For example, chambers of commerce, women's business associations, business councils, federations of industry groups (such as a federation of freight forwarders, national farmers' federations), associations of industry sectors (such as an association of textile manufacturers or automobile manufacturers). All of these are CSOs, if the organizations themselves are not-for-profit and independent of government.

Professional associations. These organizations represent the interests of their members who typically engage in a certain occupation or practice a particular profession. Professional associations may also enforce standards relating to the profession practiced by their members. Examples include associations of architects, midwives, dentists, doctors, certified public accountants, immigration agents, and economists.

Research institutes and think tanks. These organizations typically conduct research and analysis relating to public policy issues and disseminate their findings and recommendations in hopes of influencing decision-makers and opinion formers. Only nongovernment and nonprofit research institutes, universities, and colleges are CSOs (i.e., government-run universities are not CSOs). Examples include The Energy and Resources Institute and the World Resources Institute.

Social movements. These large informal groupings of individuals or organizations attempt to effect social change through sustained, organized, collective action. Social movements are not permanent institutions, but instead tend to coalesce, pursue their aims, and then dissolve. Examples include movements to end slavery, capital punishment, apartheid, and economic liberalism. The largest civil society movement calling for an end to poverty and inequality is the Global Call to Action Against Poverty.

Youth development organizations. There are many types of youth-oriented organizations, but the main distinction is between youth-led and youth-focused organizations. Youth-led organizations are typically fully staffed by young people, especially at executive level. They may include nonyouth in voluntary advisory roles. Youth-focused organizations seek as their primary objective to improve the situation of young people, but are typically staffed by people of all age groups.

In addition to the types of stand-alone CSOs described above, CSOs have converged into a wide range of coalitions or networks, united by a common geography, membership, set of objectives, or area of activity. These are often called umbrella, network, apex, or peak CSO bodies. For example, the Caucus of Development NGO Networks comprises six national networks and four regional networks representing more than 2,000 development CSOs, people's organizations, and cooperatives in the Philippines. Other examples include the Asia Venture Philanthropic Network, the Asian Labor Network on International Financial Institutions, Asian People's Exchange, South Asia Women's Network, and Voluntary Action Network India, among others.

Advocacy and operational civil society organizations. An important distinction between types of CSOs is that of operational versus advocacy CSOs. Operational CSOs directly deliver, or contribute to the delivery of, welfare services such as emergency relief or environmental protection and management. They embody a wide range of organizational structures, approaches, and areas of operation, both program-related and geographic. Operational CSOs work at the community, local, district, national, regional, and international levels. Advocacy CSOs provide representation for specific issues, concerns, points of view, or interests. They attempt to influence the policies, practices, and views of governments, development institutions like ADB, other actors in the development arena, the media, and the public at large. Examples of advocacy CSOs include the NGO Forum on ADB, PEN International, and Human Rights Watch.

This distinction is important in that it relates to the type of interaction ADB pursues with individual CSOs, such as cooperation in project implementation versus policy dialogue. The distinction also reflects the development role undertaken by these organizations. It is often impossible to neatly categorize a CSO as either an operational CSO or an advocacy CSO. This is because most CSOs are involved in a mix of operational and advocacy activities. Information on engaging with advocacy organizations is in section 5.

The civil society landscape is as diverse as society itself. It is important that ADB staff and DMC officials recognize that a community or interest group may be represented by multiple and sometimes overlapping CSOs, who may have differing opinions and views. CSOs are not homogenous, and one CSO may not be able to speak for the whole community. A specific type of CSO (e.g., youth organization, women's group) may not speak for all the target group in the project area, as there may be CSOs representing different language, ethnic, and social groupings. It is incumbent on project officers to seek a range of CSOs to engage with and to recognize that CSOs themselves are diverse and heterogenous. Section 4 provides advice on assessing the capacity of CSOs.

State-sponsored mass organizations and quasi-autonomous nongovernment organizations

Some organizations act like CSOs, and perform the roles that CSOs perform, but do not meet the criteria for being a CSO. This is particularly the case for state-sponsored mass organizations whose objectives are often to promote women's or youth empowerment, but explicitly through the lens of promoting the governing party or state's ideals. If an organization is formed by the government, and not independent from the government, then it is not a CSO. Think of it this way: a government-funded health department may conduct outreach, empower women and girls, and work closely with local communities, but this does not make it a CSO. Similarly, a state-sponsored mass organization may have deep links to communities, and perform excellent outreach and citizen engagement, but if it is formed by the government, has a reporting apparatus within the government, and is mandated to promote a particular government or governing party philosophy or ideal, it is not an independent CSO. Youth councils are examples of state-sponsored organizations which engage young people in development activities, but are part of the state youth development apparatus.

Quasi-autonomous nongovernment organizations. Quasi-autonomous NGOs (QUANGOs) are another form of CSO-like organizations. It is a particularly British abbreviation, but has relevance for Asia and the Pacific in the sense that quasi-NGOs are regularly referred to. The "quasi" part usually refers to ongoing state funding or state establishment. While many CSOs receive state funding (usually through competitive grants, tenders, project funding, and others), a quasi-NGO is not independent of government and reports to the government, and as such is not a CSO.

A final word on these organizations: although they do not meet the criteria of being independent from the state, they may also be excellent partners in ADB-financed projects, as they may have deep links to communities and other suitable attributes. But it must be remembered that these organizations are part of the state apparatus, and as such are not CSOs. An example of a state-sponsored mass organization is provided in Box 7.

The LWU was originally established in 1955 to mobilize women for the Lao People's Revolutionary Party. In 1991 the LWU was recognized under the Constitution of the Lao PDR. The LWU is mandated to "protect women's rights and interests," mobilize, and increase women's involvement in national development. The LWU is under the Party's Central Committee and plays a key role in the development of the Lao PDR government policies in regard to women and in national development. The LWU structure is represented in all ministries and reaches down to village level and has the responsibility for responding to women's development needs, promoting the status and role of women, and promoting unity among women of different ethnic groups and social strata throughout the country. The LWU at provincial and district levels is very active in livelihood development and health activities in villages. The LWU organization is often included as an implementation partner in many projects due to its already extensive network in rural communities.

Lao PDR = Lao People's Democratic Republic, LWU = Lao Women's Union.
Source: Asian Development Bank. Lao People's Democratic Republic. Health Sector Governance Program.

Approaches and Depths of Participation

ADB recognizes four main approaches to participation by stakeholders, including CSOs: (i) information generation and sharing, (ii) consultation, (iii) collaboration, and (iv) partnership. These approaches cover a continuum of relationships between decision-makers and stakeholders. The level of each party's initiative and activity differs considerably. Each approach can be explored at varying depths—low, medium, or high (Table 1). These approaches and depths of participation inform key project documents, including the initial poverty and social analysis (IPSA) and the summary poverty reduction and social strategy (SPRSS).

ADB recognizes that all ADB operations have social dimensions that need to be taken into account from country strategy formulation, programming, and project processing phases onward.[11] The IPSA and SPRSS are key project documents that must be completed as part of the poverty and social analysis (PSA). There is a clear and mandatory process for completing the PSA, which is documented in OM C3 Incorporation of Social Dimensions into ADB Operations and the *Handbook on Poverty and Social Analysis: A Working Document*, which includes guidance on how to complete the IPSA and SPRSS.[12]

As part of the process of completing the IPSA and SPRSS, staff should familiarize themselves with the approaches and depths to participation in Table 1, to factor them in during project processing and implementation and to appropriately respond to the participation and empowering the poor sections of the IPSA (part III) and SPRSS (part II).

---

[11]   ADB. 2010. Incorporation of Social Dimensions into ADB Operations. *Operations Manual*. OM C3. Manila.
[12]   ADB. 2012. *Handbook on Poverty and Social Analysis: A Working Document*. Manila.

Additionally, for the purposes of ADB's corporate results framework indicator, ADB draws its definition of meaningful CSO engagement from the approaches and depths of participation in Table 1.[13] ADB is seeking opportunities to strengthen its engagement with CSOs and has committed to reporting on whether it implements planned, "meaningful" engagement with CSOs. ADB, like other development partners, has a classification system for the approaches to participation. Projects classified as planning meaningful CSO engagement are those which exhibit these types of participation with corresponding depths as recorded in the SPRSS, part II participation and empowering the poor:

(i) Information Generation and Sharing: High
(ii) Consultation: High
(iii) Collaboration: Low, medium, or high
(iv) Partnership: Low, medium, or high (refer to Table 1)

Questions staff need to consider to determine the appropriate participatory approach for different types of projects are as follows:

Q **Does the project have scope for civil society engagement?** If the answer is **no**, consider the mandated level of *Information generation and sharing* required under ADB's Access to Information Policy (AIP). Typical projects that would fall into this category (of little scope for CSO engagement) include, but are not limited to, finance sector projects such as treasury or finance ministry strengthening, results-based or policy-based loans focused on economic reform, or strengthening the enabling environment for public–private partnerships or small and medium-sized enterprise development. However, some finance sector projects such as, but not limited to, reforming the tax base, or conditional cash transfer programs will have scope for CSO engagement.

Q **Will *consultations* with CSOs enhance project design or implementation, leading to improved development results?** Most projects will benefit from some form of consultation with CSOs, leading to a more tailored and sustainable design and implementation. If **yes**, select the preferred depth of consultation from the *Consultation* row in Table 1 (either processing or implementation column). Choose the depth of consultation that is preferred based on which depth will have the optimal improvement on project design or implementation. Remember that CSOs include industry associations, chambers of commerce, and professional associations, therefore, projects that require private sector input, such as developing technical and vocational education and training systems for improved alignment with industry needs, will benefit from CSO consultation.

Q **Will *collaboration* with CSOs enhance project design or implementation, leading to improved development results?** Consider whether there are CSOs with the capacity to collaborate (or are able to have their capacity developed for collaboration) in the project area. If there are such CSOs, and the answer to the question in bold is **yes**, select the preferred depth of collaboration from the *Collaboration* row in Table 1 (either processing or implementation column). Choose the depth of collaboration that is preferred based on what will have the optimal improvement on project design or implementation. Projects that typically benefit from collaboration with CSOs include those with a community engagement component

---

[13] Meaningful CSO engagement is defined as having the following types of participation with corresponding depths indicated in the SPRSS: high information generation and sharing; high consultation; or any level of collaboration or partnership. Further explanation of the corporate results framework indicator for CSO engagement is in section 2.

Table 1: Different Approaches and Depths of Participation

Approach	Definitions	Project Processing	Project Implementation
Information Generation and Sharing (Depth: Low, Medium, or High)	Information is ➤ generated by ADB/recipient/client and shared with CSOs; ➤ independently generated by CSOs and shared with ADB/recipient/client; or ➤ jointly produced.	**Low:** ADB/recipient/client shares information with CSOs **Medium:** Opportunities for CSOs to share information with ADB/recipient/client **High:** Joint generation and sharing of information to meet shared objectives (e.g., improved understanding)	**Low:** ADB/recipient/client shares information with CSOs **Medium:** Opportunities for CSOs to share information with ADB/recipient/client **High:** Joint generation and sharing of information to meet shared objectives (e.g., improved understanding)
Consultation (Depth: Low, Medium, or High)	CSO input is requested and considered as part of an inclusive policy, program, or project decision-making process.	**Low:** Online and/or written consultation only **Medium:** Opportunities for two-way, face-to-face exchanges (e.g., workshop, focus group) **High:** Views of CSOs incorporated into design (e.g., use participatory methods)	**Low:** Online and/or written consultation only **Medium:** Opportunities for two-way, face-to-face exchanges (e.g., workshop) **High:** Regular feedback from CSOs integrated during implementation (e.g., use participatory methods)
Collaboration (Depth: Low, Medium, or High)	CSOs and ADB/recipient/client work jointly, but CSOs have limited control over decision-making and resources.	**Low:** Inputs from specific CSOs sought in project design **Medium:** Significant CSO representation on project design body **High:** CSO influence on project design body and agreement of role for CSOs in project implementation	**Low:** CSO input in monitoring and evaluation **Medium:** Stakeholder organization (e.g., CSO) implementation of a project component[a] **High:** Significant CSO representation on project implementation body and participation in implementation activities
Partnership (Depth: Low, Medium, or High)	CSOs participate in decision-making process and/or exert control over resources through a formal or informal agreement to work together toward common objectives.	**Low:** Agree a CSO will partner in ADB-funded project **Medium:** MOU or partnership agreed, or CSOs take some degree of direct responsibility **High:** MOU or partnership agreement negotiated, including cofinancing and management; or CSOs assume high level of ownership or responsibility	**Low:** CSO routinely provides inputs and is recognized as a partner in ADB-funded project **Medium:** MOU or partnership agreement implemented, or CSOs take some degree of direct responsibility **High:** MOU or partnership agreement implemented, including financing and management; or CSOs assume high level of ownership or responsibility

ADB = Asian Development Bank, CSO = civil society organization, MOU = memorandum of understanding.
Notes: These generic definitions can be adapted to specific types of projects and programs, e.g., rural water supply; and for priority operational themes, e.g., gender or individual projects. Any segments highlighted in yellow indicate planned, meaningful CSO engagement.

[a] This includes community participation in procurement, CSOs providing consulting services, and CSOs providing nonconsulting services.

Source: Asian Development Bank.

such as, but not limited to, projects in agriculture and food security, climate change and disaster risk management, education, energy, environment, gender, health, transport, urban, and water. However, other projects that may not immediately appear to be candidates for CSO collaboration may also benefit. For example, finance sector and regional cooperation and integration (RCI) projects may benefit from CSO collaboration (for example, consider the role for CSOs in monitoring COVID-19 recovery loans, or as another example, the role of regional tourism associations in implementing regional tourism initiatives).

Q **Will *partnership* with CSOs enhance project design or implementation, leading to improved development results?** Consider whether there are CSOs with the capacity to partner (or are able to have their capacity developed for partnership) in the project area. If there are such CSOs, and the answer to the question in bold is **yes**, select the preferred depth of partnership from the *Partnership* row in Table 1 (either processing or implementation column). Choose the depth of partnership that is suitable based on what will have the optimal improvement on project design or implementation. Projects for which CSOs may partner may include, but are not be limited to, agriculture and food security (particularly farmers' cooperatives), climate change and disaster (particularly large international environment-focused CSOs and small CBOs), education (particularly nongovernment schools and colleges, and industry associations for technical and vocational education and training projects), gender (particularly national and international gender-focused CSOs, and local women's CBOs), health (particularly large international foundations), and water (particularly water user associations and national or international CSOs).

If a project has any of the above depths and approaches to participation (shaded yellow in Table 1), as recorded in the SPRSS, it is classified as having planned, meaningful CSO engagement. To calculate the CSO indicator for the corporate results framework (CRF), annually the NGO and Civil Society Center (NGOC) will review the projects which have project completion reports (PCRs) published that year. ADB will only review projects which had planned, meaningful CSO engagement. If the PCR indicates that the planned CSO engagement took place, the project will be marked as having delivered CSO engagement.

See section 2 for further information on ADB's CSO indicator under ADB's corporate results framework.

The delegation of any project implementation duties to and/or participation of CSOs under any of the four approaches to participation (i.e., information generation and sharing, consultation, collaboration, and partnership) should not pose any limitations to the Office of Anticorruption and Integrity's mandate to conduct proactive integrity reviews on ADB-financed, -administered, and/or -supported projects. The audit clause in the loan or grant agreement with the borrower should extend to the CSOs involved, as appropriate. As such, the memoranda of understanding or agreements signed with CSOs should include a language that allows ADB and/or its representatives to inspect the project, goods, and any relevant records and documents.

Some notes on how to interpret Table 1

The important and often overlooked aspect of Table 1 is the definitions column. Start with this column to determine the approach to participation, and then move to the processing or implementation columns, as appropriate. Within the appropriate column (processing or implementation), select Low, Medium, or High (or not applicable) from within the selected participation approach row (i.e., information generation and sharing, consultation, collaboration, partnership).

Q **What does Collaboration – Medium "implementation of a project component" mean?**
CSO implementation of a project component often refers to project components delivered by a CSO in a consulting firm or service provider capacity (e.g., implementation of safeguards plans or gender action plans), and thus governed by procurement policy and regulations covering community participation in recruitment, consulting services and nonconsulting services. CSOs may also deliver a project component in a voluntary capacity, without payment, and while rare, this is also classified as Collaboration Medium. For Collaboration Medium, the CSO has no input on the broader direction of the project, beyond the scope of that project component (or components, if they are delivering several).

Q **What about if there is a CSO representative on the project steering committee or advisory group and they are also implementing a project component?**
Collaboration – High is described as "Significant CSO representation on a project implementation body and participation in implementation activities": this means the CSO has both a formal role in the implementation arrangements plus is delivering one or some project components, hence, it presents a greater depth of engagement than Collaboration – Medium delivering project component(s).

Q **How is the distinction between Collaboration and Partnership determined?**
Look at the definition column. CSO implementation of a project component typically refers to when a CSO is in a consulting firm or service provider role. In these situations, the CSO implementing the project component does not participate in a partnership role with ADB or the DMC government (or client/borrower)—they are contracted as consulting firms or service providers or providing voluntary services. They have "limited control over decision-making and resources" (part of the collaboration definition) except for responsibilities, resources, and/or decision-making within the scope of their allocated project component(s).

The definition of partnership indicates they have a broader level of control, in partnership with ADB and the DMC government (or client/borrower), over the overall project direction, resources, and decision-making, beyond just specific project components. Partnership may be defined by a document outlining the roles and responsibilities of each of the parties.

Q **Under Consultation, what about the challenges brought about by the COVID-19 pandemic and cases where face-to-face consultation is not possible?**
In this situation, consider "face-to-face" to also mean utilizing alternate online interactive platforms. Online forums can be highly interactive, but be aware of who is unable to attend due to the format. Those CSOs representing the poor, vulnerable, and excluded, along with smaller CSOs, may not be able to participate (e.g., if they have limited resources, poor electricity and low or no internet access). See Box 15 for more on online consultations with CSOs.

Refer to section 2 for how to complete the SPRSS, part II, participation and empowering the poor.

For more discussion and templates on participation in ADB-financed activities, read ADB's *Handbook on Poverty and Social Analysis: A Working Document* with further guidance in ADB's *Strengthening Participation for Development Results: An Asian Development Bank Guide to Participation.*

2

Policy and Operations

Roles for Civil Society Organizations in ADB-Financed Operations

Under Strategy 2030, the Asian Development Bank (ADB) aims to achieve a prosperous, inclusive, resilient, and sustainable Asia and the Pacific. To achieve this vision, ADB has seven operational priority (OP) areas. Civil society organizations (CSOs) can make important contributions to each of these operational areas. The seven areas are as follows:

(i) OP1: Addressing remaining poverty and reducing inequalities.
(ii) OP2: Accelerating progress in gender equality.
(iii) OP3: Tackling climate change, building climate and disaster resilience, and enhancing environmental sustainability.
(iv) OP4: Making cities more livable.
(v) OP5: Promoting rural development and food security.
(vi) OP6: Strengthening governance and institutional capacity.
(vii) OP7: Fostering regional cooperation and integration.

ADB's Strategy 2030 states that ADB "will strengthen collaboration with civil society organizations designing, implementing, and monitoring projects."[14] ADB seeks to strengthen CSO engagement to improve access of the poor, vulnerable, and excluded groups to food, energy, transport, clean water, and sanitation services; and address issues such as addressing poverty, reducing inequalities, advancing gender equality, accessing microfinance, environmental protection, and tackling climate change.

Appendix 1 details potential contributions that CSOs can make to achieving ADB's seven operational priorities.

Preparing or Reviewing a Policy with Civil Society Organization Engagement

ADB's policy development and policy reviews provide significant scope for CSO engagement. ADB recognizes the importance of seeking the guidance of internal and external stakeholders, as appropriate, during the processing of policy or strategy papers. Input received through consultation with civil society is constructive and valuable and reflects a variety of alternative views and perspectives. ADB should seek CSO input on major policy and strategy papers,[15] as relevant, and depending on the required approach and depth of participation in Table 1.[16]

The development of major policy and strategy papers should include consultations with international and regional CSOs and country-level consultations with relevant CSOs, as appropriate. ADB should endeavor

---

[14] Footnote 3. p. vii.
[15] ADB seeks the participation of its shareholders and other interested stakeholders during the development and review of safeguard, sector, and thematic policies and strategies; and other policies or strategies that will undergo public consultation.
[16] Footnote 3, para. 108.

to seek external input on policy and strategy papers involving safeguards. In addition to dialogue with civil society and consultation to address specific issues, ADB should maintain and/or implement mechanisms for regular policy-level consultation and dialogue with CSOs. Consultations should facilitate effective two-way communication on policy-related topics, and be positive, proactive, and mutually beneficial.[17] The NGO and Civil Society Center (NGOC) can assist with the planning and execution of such CSO consultations.

The objective of the review and consultation process is to consider the views of all stakeholders and to ensure they have every opportunity to be involved in developing ADB policy and strategy. This will help make sure the final version of a document reflects best international practices and has engaged all the concerned parties.

External consultation should be seen as an opportunity to benefit from the knowledge and experience of others and to strengthen their ownership in the process. Take care not to overlook the potential for CSOs to play a facilitating role in policy making.

For policies relating to safeguards, external consultation is essential. In the case of other policies and strategies, particularly those relating to sector or thematic areas, external consultation is encouraged. However, a policy or strategy paper relating to budgeting or administration that only concerns ADB's internal workings needs no external consultation.

While external consultations are not required in all cases, consulting external stakeholders, including CSOs, in the review of policies and strategies generally produces outcomes that
- (i)   are technically superior to documents prepared without the benefit of external consultations,
- (ii)   are more relevant to the context of ADB's developing member countries (DMCs),
- (iii) incorporate internationally accepted best practices,
- (iv)   improve understanding of ADB's objectives and operations,
- (v)   consider a broad base of information and range of perspectives,
- (vi)   are harmonized with government and other development partner policies, and
- (vii) enjoy greater support by a wider range of stakeholders.

Examples of ADB policies and strategies prepared with extensive consultations include Strategy 2030, country partnership strategies, Energy Policy 2021, Access to Information Policy 2019, the Accountability Mechanism Policy 2012, and the Safeguard Policy Statement (2009).

In general, the guidelines for effective consultations advise to
- (i)   plan early, share the plan, and plan updates;
- (ii)   develop a thorough stakeholder analysis;
- (iii)   design a cost-effective consultation and participation plan based on the stakeholder analysis;
- (iv)   develop a communications strategy (see next para. for guidance);
- (v)   use skilled facilitators;
- (vi)   allow sufficient time for review of the document;
- (vii)   offer stakeholders opportunities to discuss the document in draft form; and
- (viii) share feedback with participants so they understand how ADB used their inputs.

As part of policy preparation or review, develop a communication strategy and consider these key elements:

---

[17]   ADB. 1998. *Cooperation Between Asian Development Bank and Nongovernment Organizations*. Manila.

(i) create online platforms to serve as central information hub (i.e., webpage such as the Safeguard Policy Statement review website), social media pages to drive traffic to webpage and facilitate interactive exchanges;

(ii) use stakeholder analysis to determine and use other communication channels to generate feedback and distribute content;

(iii) clarify feedback loops—how stakeholder feedback is documented, addressed, and integrated within a timeframe;

(iv) develop communication materials in popular formats to unpack technical details of documents, and visual aids for consultations;

(v) develop frequently asked questions (FAQs), talking points, and briefing notes for consistency in tone and messaging; and

(vi) develop crisis communication approaches to anticipate and respond to potential reputational issues.

Good practice in engaging civil society organizations in policy development and review

ADB follows these steps when developing or reviewing policies and strategies using a consultative approach, noting that the consultation process will consist of some or all of these steps and approaches described below, depending on the nature of the policy or strategy:

(i) Undertake a stakeholder analysis to determine which groups or individuals will best contribute to the review process and draft a consultation and participation plan that describes how ADB and the DMC government will engage with stakeholders. Provide the draft plan to the NGOC for review and input, as NGOC is aware of the types of issues and concerns that CSOs may raise about the draft plan.

(ii) Confer with internal and external groups that have specialized knowledge or have a particular interest in the policy or strategy being developed or reviewed.

(iii) Create a website for the review process that publicizes details about how the review will be conducted and how interested persons or organizations can contribute. An example of such a website is the Safeguard Policy Review.[18]

(iv) Make at least two drafts of the proposed policy or strategy available for public comment during the review and give stakeholders enough time to comment on the drafts. Be sure to indicate if comments will be posted publicly, with permission.

(v) Translate the proposal into appropriate languages, as relevant, and consider producing alternative representations of the policy such as youth-friendly or graphical versions.

(vi) Use communication channels, in addition to the ADB website, to invite comments and to announce the beginning and end dates of the comment period.

(vii) Organize face-to-face consultations at the country or subregional level in a geographically diverse group of member countries.

(viii) Develop invitation lists together with the resident mission in the country concerned, government bodies, and ADB's NGOC. In developing the invitation list, take care to make sure CSOs representing vulnerable, marginalized, or excluded groups are included. Depending on the context, this can include women, people with disabilities, young people, older people, migrants, LGBT+ people, and other vulnerable, marginalized, or excluded groups.

(ix) Make drafts of the proposed policy or strategy available to workshop participants at least 30 days in advance of the consultation, preferably in the national language of the country concerned.

(x) Carry out online consultations in parallel with face-to-face consultations.

---

[18] ADB. Safeguard Policy Review.

(xi)   Post stakeholder comments on the website (with permission) along with an explanation of how comments have been considered in revised versions of the proposed policy or strategy (e.g., by preparing a comments matrix).

(xii)   Promptly post any changes to the review process on the review website (e.g., details relating to workshop arrangements or extensions of the review process).

Staff members responsible for implementing the policy or strategy can help identify stakeholders, as can the CSO anchors at resident missions and representative offices. These specialists have an advantage in awareness-raising activities at the country level and can make positive contributions to the review.

For more discussion and templates on participation in policy review and formulation, read Chapter 2 of ADB's *Strengthening Participation for Development Results: An Asian Development Bank Guide to Participation.*[19]

Engaging Civil Society Organizations during Country Programming

The country partnership strategy (CPS)[20] continues to serve as a primary relationship document between a DMC and ADB. It sets out shared priorities and strengthens the mutual ownership of ADB's public and private sector assistance program. As part of the CPS preparation, country consultations should be undertaken. As needed, CSOs should be consulted as part of these country consultations throughout the CPS process.[21]

ADB places importance on working with CSOs to tap their unique strengths, such as their local presence and specialized knowledge, and commits to exploring opportunities for increasing their involvement in the design and implementation of projects supported by ADB.[22] For this reason, in forming CPSs, "ADB will consult with citizens, civil society, and the private sector to promote responsive governance and improved service delivery."[23] This consultative process should be part of a broader assessment of CSO presence and capacities in the DMC, and the identification of opportunities for increasing citizen and CSO engagement, focusing on key sectors. The assessment will inform, and can form part of, the governance risk assessment under the Second Governance and Anticorruption Action Plan and should provide a pathway for meaningful citizen and CSO engagement within the DMC, which can then be monitored and measured at the country, sector, and project levels.[24]

As appropriate, ADB staff will work with key government officials to facilitate the engagement of CSOs during CPS preparation.[25] To encourage CSO engagement in the development of the CPS, background information on the CPS and the draft CPS should be shared for input, as available.[26] For consultations on the draft CPS, copies should be made available in advance to in-country stakeholders for comment.[27] Principles of meaningful consultation with civil society should be used during country and regional programming.

---

[19]   ADB. 2012. *Strengthening Participation for Development Results: An Asian Development Bank Guide to Participation.* Manila.
[20]   References to the CPS include the regional cooperation strategy.
[21]   ADB. 2016. Country Partnership Strategy. *Operations Manual.* OM A2. Manila.
[22]   Footnote 16.
[23]   ADB. 2019. *Strategy 2030 Operational Plan for Priority 6: Strengthening Governance and Institutional Capacity, 2019–2024.* Manila.
[24]   ADB. 2006. *Second Governance and Anticorruption Action Plan (GACAP II).* Manila.
[25]   Footnote 11.
[26]   ADB. 2019. Access to Information Policy. *Operations Manual.* OM L3. Manila.
[27]   Footnote 11.

CPS preparation and implementation is an ideal opportunity to engage with CSOs in country. However, an information session where CSOs come to the ADB office, watch a presentation on the draft plan, and then are given an opportunity to ask questions rarely adds value to the document. A good strategy is to identify where and when CSO inputs would be valuable and then plan how to solicit them from the organizations who have the relevant expertise. Consider some of the following activities to incorporate CSO engagement into the CPS process:

(i) Prepare a stakeholder mapping analysis of CSOs in the country and understand who could contribute to the CPS and the achievement of the CPS' implementation priorities, and how meaningful citizen and CSO engagement can support such priorities at the country, sector, and agency levels during the CPS life cycle. Start with engaging with the CSO anchor who may keep a database of active CSOs; reach out to umbrella networks of CSOs or coalitions to help identify key CSOs in the relevant sectors. For more discussion and templates on participation and stakeholder analysis, read Tool 1 (stakeholder analysis and consultation) of ADB's *Strengthening Participation for Development Results: An Asian Development Bank Guide to Participation*.

(ii) Prepare an assessment of the government's transparency and level of engagement with CSOs and citizens, especially in key sectors, as part of a governance risk assessment. Examples of tools to assist in the preparation of such an assessment are included in the external resources section of this guide (Appendix 2). This will include an achievable, monitorable, and measurable plan to ensure adequate transparency and CSO/citizen engagement during the CPS cycle. Consider sharing this assessment with local stakeholders for verification and input, if appropriate.

(iii) Refer to ADB's Civil Society Briefs series for an overview of the civil society landscape in a country where available, but also use apex organizations in the country as entry points to understand the civil society landscape.

(iv) Combine country team retreats with participatory stakeholder consultations and use them to introduce the basic CPS procedures, identify lessons from previous projects, and develop consensus on country development issues.

(v) Consider how inclusive and participatory the CPS processes will be: identify how the voices of disabled people, children and youth, the poor, vulnerable, and excluded will be incorporated into the CPS process.

(vi) Prepare for the CPS formulation process through consultations, meetings, and workshops with stakeholders in the government, development partners, CSOs, academics, and the private sector or consider seeking sector-specific CSO inputs. The consultations and workshops may feed into the country diagnostics and assessments which may feed into the inclusive and sustainable growth assessment. For example, an ADB resident mission set up CSO focus groups to provide inputs to inclusive and sustainable growth assessments of three sectors. These three focus groups reviewed and commented on early sector assessment drafts.

(vii) Prepare a background document on CSO activity to inform the CPS process. Use it to inform the way CSOs can contribute to the development of the CPS.

(viii) Invite CSOs to meetings during the CPS formulation mission.

(ix) **Facilitate high-quality consultations**. Ensure good practice in consultations, including inviting participants well in advance, sharing background information in advance and in a language understood by participants, selecting a meeting venue or technology format where participants will feel comfortable, and seeking relevant sector or geographic coverage. Identify a few questions that will focus the discussions for which CSO inputs will be genuinely valuable. Refer to section 3 on principles for effective consultation with CSOs.

(x) **Engage a civil society organization representative as a peer reviewer**. Representatives from CSO umbrella organizations or working group participants may make useful peer reviewers.

(xi)   **Conduct a desk review of civil society organization literature and data in the country**. CSOs in some countries generate a substantial number of reports and analyses that could help validate other sources and or complement existing data.

(xii)   **Develop a measurable and achievable plan on citizen and civil society organization engagement for the country partnership strategy**. Make sure it includes consideration of how information will reach CSOs about the timeline and opportunities to comment online and during meetings. For more discussion and templates on participation plans, read Tool 4 (developing a participation plan) in ADB's *Strengthening Participation for Development Results: An Asian Development Bank Guide to Participation*.

(xiii)   **Document the CSO engagement process during CPS preparation**. The Lao People's Democratic Republic (Lao PDR) resident mission[28] and the Nepal resident mission[29] have both done this, and both examples are on the ADB and Civil Society website.

For more discussion and templates on participation in the CPS, read Chapter 2 of ADB's *Strengthening Participation for Development Results: An Asian Development Bank Guide to Participation*.

Engaging with Civil Society Organizations in the Project Cycle

ADB encourages engagement with CSOs in formulating, designing, implementing, monitoring, and evaluating projects, where appropriate.[30] To complement its core activities, ADB continues to strengthen its engagement with CSOs by sharing knowledge and expertise.[31] ADB is committed to exploring opportunities for increasing CSO involvement in the design and implementation of projects, especially on those projects and technical assistance (TA) operations using grassroots and participatory approaches.[32] CSOs are part of a regional department's due diligence process from project design through Board approval.

ADB's experience is that involving CSOs improves the quality of projects by promoting inclusiveness and placing citizens at the center of the development process.[33]

Early engagement and communication with CSOs in the project cycle are critical for exploring opportunities for CSO participation in ADB-financed operations. Communication plays a vital role in CSO engagement in various stages of the project cycle, from project preparation to project closing. But it is at the project preparation stage that CSO engagement should be considered. Complex projects in particular will benefit from a well-planned communication strategy designed during project preparation and due diligence, particularly if CSOs are identified as a key stakeholder during stakeholder analysis.

CSOs may be engaged at the project level on ADB-financed projects in multiple ways, and this section details this. Figure 3 provides an overview of entry points for CSO engagement throughout the ADB project cycle.

---

[28]   ADB. 2017. *Voices for Inclusive and Sustainable Growth. Lao PDR Country Partnership Strategy Civil Society Stakeholder Consultation*. Manila.
[29]   ADB. 2013. *Voices from the Field. Nepal Country Partnership Strategy Stakeholder Consultations*. Manila.
[30]   Footnote 11.
[31]   ADB. 2017. Development Partnerships. *Operations Manual*. OM E3. Manila.
[32]   Footnote 16.
[33]   Footnote 23.

Figure 3: Overview of Civil Society Organization Engagement in the Project Cycle

CSOs may participate in CPS formulation and review, including sector assessments and the inclusive and sustainable growth assessment. Teams may consult CSOs in the development of a CPS.

CSOs may participate in the design of projects either as consultants or service providers, or through project design consultations (as representatives or target groups). They may also perform advocacy roles. Planning for CSO engagement in implementation occurs at this point.

CSOs may participate in the project completion or evaluation as consultants/service providers or through independent review. Review missions may consult CSOs.

ADB Project Cycle

Country Partnership Strategy Regional Cooperation Strategy

Preparation

Approval

Implementation

Completion/ Evaluation

CSOs do not have a role in project approval. However, ADB posts the approved projects on the ADB website and CSOs may monitor them as part of their advocacy efforts.

CSOs may participate in the implementation of projects as implementing entities, consultants, services providers, target groups, beneficiaries, or monitors (either as a consultant/service provider or independently). They may comment on implementation in their roles as advocacy organizations.

ADB = Asian Development Bank, CPS = country partnership strategy, CSO = civil society organization.
Source: Asian Development Bank

27

Civil society organizations as implementing entities

CSOs may be implementing entities[34] for ADB-financed operations, with the concurrence of the DMC government. Regional departments may ask the government to engage CSOs to perform these roles in fragile and conflict-affected situations (FCAS). Under grants financed by the Japan Fund for Prosperous and Resilient Asia and the Pacific (JFPR), CSOs may be executing agencies.[35] In engaging with any organization, staff should check the financial, integrity, and reputational aspects of due diligence.[36] Integrity due diligence is mandatory for any executing agency or implementing agency that is not a government ministry or agency. Financial due diligence is required for all executing and implementing agencies, and for CSOs where they assume the role of an implementing entity, to assess whether financial management processes ensure accountability, efficiency, economy, and solvency.

When a CSO is an implementing entity, ADB staff should ensure that the CSO is familiar with ADB's Anticorruption Policy and the requirements to access and check ADB's sanctions list, as appropriate.[37] CSOs should also understand where, how, and what to report if there is an integrity concern or allegation of integrity violation on an ADB-related activity.

The following is an example of a CSO performing the role of an implementing entity.

BOX 8

Partnership with a CSO in Transforming the Lives of Low-income Women-Microentrepreneurs and their Families

ASA Philippines Foundation (ASA),[a] a microfinance institution–nongovernment organization, received a $30 million credit facility from ADB to support women micro-entrepreneurs from economically lagging, environmentally impacted, and conflict-affected provinces in the Philippines. With initial funds from its benefactors, ASA continues to be a not-for-profit organization providing financial services to 1.9 million underprivileged clients through its 1,683 branches located across 82 provinces. ASA helps women from low-income families to establish or improve their microenterprises through uncollateralized small loans and small savings as capital build-ups. Aside from improving family income, ASA is also committed to improving the lives of its clients and their families through micro-housing loans for home refurbishment and strengthening, installation of solar electricity, and water and sanitation facilities. ASA's Client Community Service Program, with funds sourced from operations austerity measures, also provides direct benefits to clients and families by offering college or university scholarship programs, burial and hospitalization assistance, disaster relief and rehabilitation assistance, business development training, and marketing support, among others. ADB's financing reinforces ASA's endeavor to achieve inclusive financing and lift Filipino families out of poverty. In 2019, at least 78% of ASA's borrowers increased their income, savings, and assets; 7% of supported enterprises created 258,052 jobs; and 90% of borrowers sent their children (16-year-old and above) to school.

ADB = Asian Development Bank, CSO = civil society organization.
[a] ASA Philippines Foundation. 2019. *Annual Report 2019: To the Nanays for Their Trust*. Manila.
Source: Asian Development Bank.

---

[34] The term "implementing agency" is typically used to refer to government agencies that are responsible for implementing one or more components of a project. Where third parties are engaged to help the government carry out those activities (and are remunerated for it), this sourcebook refers to them as "implementing entities" to distinguish them from the implementing agencies that are typically associated with government agencies.
[35] ADB. 2011. Japan Fund for Poverty Reduction. *Operations Manual*. OM E2. Manila.
[36] ADB. 2014. Financial Management, Cost Estimates, Financial Analysis, and Financial Performance Indicators. *Operations Manual*. OM G2. Manila.
[37] ADB. 1998. *Anticorruption: Our Framework Policies and Strategies*. Manila.

Working with civil society organizations during project processing

CSOs typically play two main roles during project processing, where appropriate: (i) participating in consultations about the project design; and (ii) participating as consultants (firm or individuals)[38] or service providers, where the CSOs provide technical inputs to inform the project design. In addition, they may also perform advocacy roles during project processing.

Civil society organization engagement in project design consultations

When CSOs participate in consultations during project design, they may represent the interest of their constituents or be a target group of potential project activities.

These CSOs may be those that

(i)   provide services to the poor and vulnerable, such as welfare provider CSOs, faith-based groups, disability providers, irrigation groups, youth groups, women's refuges or CSOs who engage in advocacy, and/or provide services to survivors of gender-based and domestic violence;

(ii)   represent organizations or professionals in the project area such as local chambers of commerce, business women's associations, unions, guilds, or professional associations (of engineers, teachers, health workers, and others); and/or

(iii)   are groupings of CSOs, such as disability support CSO groups, umbrella groups of women and youth, or peak network CSO bodies in a country may also participate in project design activities.

Stakeholder consultations for results-based lending programs, including indicative disbursement-linked indicators, draft fiduciary system assessments, and draft environmental and social systems assessment should include CSOs.[39] Advocacy CSOs, including anti-debt groups and anticorruption organizations, may also be consulted as part of project due diligence. See section 3 for principles of effective consultations with CSOs.

Meaningful civil society organization consultations for safeguards compliance in project design

Where applicable, meaningful consultation with CSOs will be conducted in accordance with ADB's Safeguard Policy Statement.[40] ADB will require borrowers or clients to engage with CSOs through information disclosure, consultation, and informed participation in a manner commensurate with the project's risks and impacts. Such consultation requires the involvement of concerned CSOs early in project preparation. It is carried out throughout the project cycle, and ensures their views are taken into consideration in a project's environmental and social performance.

ADB's Safeguard Policy Statement contains more detail on meaningful consultations during project design.

---

[38]   An individual consultant or service provider is normally selected based on his or her qualifications, rather than an affiliation with a specific CSO.

[39]   ADB. 2019. *Mainstreaming Results-Based Lending for Programs*. Manila.

[40]   ADB. 2009. *Safeguard Policy Statement*. Manila.

Engaging civil society organizations as beneficiaries or target groups of potential project activities

In some instances, CSOs may be the direct beneficiaries or be a target group of potential project activities. This particularly occurs when ADB-financed projects aim to strengthen CBOs or grassroots organizations such as water user groups, women's self-help groups, and farmers' cooperatives. However, other types of CSOs may also be the target of ADB-financed projects, for example, industry associations, youth-led organizations, or civil society microfinance organizations. In these cases, the CSO participates in project design consultations as a potential direct beneficiary of the project, rather than as a representative of beneficiaries.

BOX 9

Many ADB-financed programs and projects include in their performance indicators and targets the participation and benefits of CSOs or CBOs. For example, as highlighted in a study conducted by the South Asia Department:

"A notable feature of ADB projects that work with CBOs is the consistent effort to support women's participation and leadership. For example, the Crop Diversification Project in Bangladesh aims for 30% participation of women among farmers mobilized into groups. The Community-Managed Irrigated Agriculture Project in Nepal aims for 33% participation by women in water user associations and the Sri Lanka Secondary Towns and Rural Water Supply and Sanitation Projects aimed for 50% representation of women in participating CBOs. In many cases, a large part of the responsibility in achieving these targets rests with the CSOs engaged to conduct social mobilization and group formation. These initiatives help promote women's access to information related to project and sector objectives as well as access to benefits and resources associated with participation. They are also important in helping women learn skills that can be used in other settings, building confidence, and reinforcing the legitimacy of women's participation in economic activities and community decision-making, in accordance with gender equality principles endorsed by ADB and partner countries."

However, not all CSOs who are target groups are CBOs. In Timor-Leste, ADB supported the strengthening of the Timor Coffee Association (ACT) under a TA grant. ACT is a trade association that represents the interests of stakeholders at each stage of the coffee value chain. ACT was supported under the TA by consultants from the Coffee Quality Institute, which is a nonprofit organization working internationally to improve the quality of coffee. The main TA output was the development of the Timor-Leste National Coffee Sector Development Plan (2019–2030), which was launched by the minister of agriculture in May 2019. This example demonstrates both the CSO as a target group (the Timor Coffee Association), and the use of another CSO (the Coffee Quality Institute) to provide consulting services to support ACT.

ADB = Asian Development Bank, CBO = community-based organization, CSO = civil society organization, TA = technical assistance.
Sources: ADB. 2015. *How Does ADB Engage Civil Society Organizations in its Operations? Findings of an Exploratory Inquiry in South Asia.* Manila; ADB. 2019. *Technical Assistance Completion Report: Support for Preparation of a National Coffee Sector Development Plan for Timor-Leste.* Manila.

Engaging civil society organizations in project design for transactional technical assistance

CSOs may be engaged in consultations under transaction TA or as consulting firms or service providers under transaction TA.

(i) **CSO engaged in consultations under transaction technical assistance**

Engaging with CSOs, with their deep links to communities, knowledge, and experience of participatory and grassroots approaches, and in some cases, as subject matter experts (e.g., with expertise in community education in water, sanitation, and hygiene [WASH], or a deep understanding of issues of governance and transparency, gender-based violence [GBV] and risks of sexual exploitation, abuse and harassment [SEAH], youth development, conservation, forestry, environment, climate change, agriculture, and others), should be part of the due diligence process that staff undertake during project design. Engaging with CSOs can strengthen participation and improve accountability.[41]

(ii) **CSO engaged as consulting firms or service providers under transaction technical assistance**

CSOs may be recruited as consulting firms or service providers to support transaction TA. The business processes for recruiting CSOs in these situations are similar to those used for the recruitment of consulting firms.

When CSOs are engaged as consultants or service providers in project design, they may provide a range of services. These tasks may include designing, facilitating and/or leading community consultations, conducting surveys, or providing enumerators for surveys (e.g., willingness-to-pay surveys, road safety awareness scans, work on indigenous people's plans, and others), providing specific intelligence or market analysis (e.g., value chain analysis, sector report on community health posts, and others) and other similar clearly defined tasks.

BOX 10

Under the Republic of Armenia: Water Supply and Sanitation Sector Project,[a] the Aarhus Centers facilitated consultation with 19 CSOs in Armenia during project preparation. Through these consultations, CSOs' concerns were considered. The consultations also provided CSOs with the opportunity to object to elements of the project design. Engaging with a wide range of stakeholders reportedly helped ease relations across project stakeholder groups.

CSO = civil society organization.
[a] ADB. Republic of Armenia: Water Supply and Sanitation Sector Project.
Source: Asian Development Bank.

ADB and DMC staff implementing ADB-financed projects should consider the capacity of CSOs to conduct work under transaction TA. Some CSOs, particularly local or grassroots organizations, may need capacity support to perform these roles, as described in Box 11.

---

[41] ADB. 2010. Governance. *Operations Manual*. OM C4. Manila.

In Kiribati, the project team for the South Tarawa Water Supply Sector Project consulted with local and international CSOs on project design.[a] International CSOs included Live and Learn Environmental Education, Child Fund, and the Red Cross. Consultations also included Te Maeu, a local CSO. Two local CSOs, Te Maeu and Kiribati Community Health Organization, participated in training to build their capacity to support community consultations during project design. The two local CSOs, working with the project design advance firm, planned and facilitated a series of community workshops to gain insights into community preferences on the project plans.

See section 4 for more information on CSO engagement in procurement.

CSO = civil society organization.
[a] ADB. Kiribati: South Tarawa Water Supply Project.
Source: Asian Development Bank.

Preparing a design and monitoring framework

In designing a project, staff should use participatory approaches to prepare the project design and monitoring framework (DMF). CSOs are key stakeholders in this participatory foundation of DMF preparation, as project design benefits from engagement of key stakeholders, including beneficiaries.[42] Entry points for CSO engagement in DMF preparation are stakeholder analysis, theory of change, inputs, indicators, and data sources.

Consider the roles that CSOs may play, and the perspectives they bring, when preparing the DMF, particularly when preparing these components:

(i) **Stakeholder analysis.** Along with other stakeholder groups (beneficiaries, public sector, private sector), staff should consider CSOs in the stakeholder analysis. Staff should include a category for CSO stakeholders in the DMF stakeholder analysis. CSO representatives can also be participants in participatory workshops to frame the stakeholder analysis.

(ii) **Theory of change.** When undertaking a situation analysis, CSOs and other stakeholders should be directly engaged in the problem analysis, using participatory approaches suitable to the local context. The problem analysis informs the theory of change, and good project design is based on an evidence-based theory of change, developed in consultation with key stakeholders, including CSOs.

(iii) **Inputs.** The inputs are resources that the project requires to achieve the outputs. Staff should list CSO inputs (financial and, for TA, in-kind inputs) if they are engaged on an ADB-financed project. Inputs from CSOs should be listed in the DMF in the inputs column and grouped by financier (including CSOs, as relevant). CSO inputs often will be in-kind and nonfinancial.

(iv) **Indicators.** Staff should consider stakeholder perspectives where appropriate, especially from beneficiaries (and their representative CSOs), to specify indicators and set targets.

(v) **Data sources.** CSOs may provide the data source (primary and/or secondary) for DMF indicators.[43] CSOs may also be a source for sex-disaggregated data, including for baselines, for gender designs in the DMF and gender action plans (GAPs).

---

[42] ADB. 2020. *Guidelines for Preparing and Using a Design and Monitoring Framework: Sovereign Operations and Technical Assistance.* Manila.
[43] Footnote 42.

For discussion on the participatory basis of the DMF and the role for CSOs, read ADB's 2020 *Guidelines for Preparing and Using a Design and Monitoring Framework: Sovereign Operations and Technical Assistance.*

For more discussion and templates on participation in DMF preparation, read Tool 2 (maximizing participation in the DMF) of ADB's *Strengthening Participation for Development Results: An Asian Development Bank Guide to Participation.*

Documenting civil society organization engagement during project processing

As outlined in section 1, ADB recognizes that all ADB operations have social dimensions that need to be taken into account from country strategy formulation, programming, and project processing phases onward.[44] The process for completing the poverty and social analysis (PSA) is documented in OM C3 and the *Handbook on Poverty and Social Analysis: A Working Document.*[45] The process involves project teams articulating via the initial poverty and social analysis (IPSA) how they will conduct the PSA and what are some of the key issues that will need to be addressed in project processing. A project concept paper will include an IPSA as part of the PSA, of which CSO engagement is one component. After concept clearance, project teams and consultant resources undertake the PSA, involving consultation, assessment, and analysis (of all of the social and poverty issues, of which CSO engagement is only a small part). More information on the requirements for conducting PSA is available in *Handbook on Poverty and Social Analysis: A Working Document,* which also includes guidance on how to complete the IPSA and how the IPSA is key in the PSA process.[46]

In sovereign loans and grants, staff must complete the IPSA at the concept phase. The participation and empowering the poor section of the IPSA describes key features, responsibilities, and resources to strengthen the participation of CSOs and/or the poor and vulnerable.[47] The IPSA must be disclosed to the public upon approval of the project or program concept note for sovereign projects, and upon completion of credit approval for nonsovereign projects.[48]

Staff must detail under the IPSA, part III participation and empowering the poor, what the key CSOs are in the project area and what is the level of CSO participation in project design. Staff must also indicate the participatory approaches planned for project design, and the depth of those approaches, using Table 1.

When completing the IPSA, staff may consider and articulate the way that CSOs may assist in project processing. For example, by representing different segments of society or by organizing the participation of the wider population of whom they are a part. Special consideration needs to be given to how poor, vulnerable, and excluded groups may participate in project design consultations, or if held online, how they will participate, and what additional support is required to allow inclusive participation. Attention needs to be paid to engaging with the representative organizations of the poor, vulnerable, and excluded, such as organizations of people with disabilities (OPDs), identity organizations, older people's organizations, and those representing the marginalized.

---

[44] Footnote 11.
[45] Footnote 12.
[46] Footnote 12.
[47] Footnote 12. For definitions of "poor" and "vulnerable" refer to the glossary and ADB Results Framework Indicator Definitions. ADB. 2021. *Results Framework Indicator Definitions.* Manila.
[48] Footnote 26. The guideline for disclosure of the IPSA is outlined in OM L3.

BOX 12

The situation in the SARD member countries demand that both GESI be pursued to ensure that intersecting inequalities experienced by different excluded and vulnerable groups based on gender; age; disability; social identities (e.g., caste, ethnicity, and religion); sexual and gender identities; geographic location; and income status are reduced. Excluded are those people who have historically experienced systemic disadvantage, while vulnerable are those who experience situational disadvantage. Gender inequality is a core part of all forms of exclusion and vulnerability, with women of disadvantaged groups (e.g., women with disabilities, of caste or ethnic minority groups, older women) experiencing compounded barriers. The SARD GESI framework recognizes the multiple layers of disadvantage arising from intersectionality and intersecting identities. Hence, the elements of the GESI framework are (i) to understand, that is to identify who are the excluded and vulnerable, the causes, and existing responses; (ii) to empower for livelihood and voice empowerment; and (iii) to include, that is to reduce discriminatory formal and informal policies and systems. CSOs and civil society have a key role in informing, mobilizing, and enhancing the skills of the excluded and vulnerable people, fostering reflection by both those with and without power and facilitating evidence-based influencing of policy makers. They can foster reflection on inequitable issues by both, those with and those without power, and facilitate evidence-based influencing of policy makers for gender equality, women's empowerment, and social inclusion.

CSO = civil society organization, GESI = gender equality and social inclusion, SARD = South Asia Department.
Source: Asian Development Bank.

Table 2: Sample Responses Initial Poverty and Social Analysis, Part III

III. PARTICIPATION AND EMPOWERING THE POOR
1. Who are the main stakeholders of the project, including beneficiaries and affected people? Explain how they will each participate in the project's design. Stakeholders include the Water Authority, the Ministry of Finance and Treasury, CSOs (including WaterAID, Live and Learn, and World Vision), development partners, landowners, households, and businesses in the project area. CSOs will be engaged to facilitate consultation with communities in the project area.
2. Who are the key, active, and relevant CSOs in the project area? Some of CSOs that may be consulted or requested to collaborate in the project design include churches and church groups, Development Services Exchange, Solomon Islands National Council of Women, and the Solomon Islands Chamber of Commerce and Industries.
3. Are there issues during project design for which participation of the poor and vulnerable is important? ☒ Yes   ☐ No   If yes, what are these issues? A key design feature of the project is the intense community engagement that will be carried out during all stages of project design and implementation and which will set targets for engagement with low-income households and other vulnerable groups. The project's hygiene awareness and education program component will involve training local CSOs to lead the program, including spreading messages on good hygiene, household water treatment, and safe storage and sanitation practices. In project design, the capacity of local CSOs to deliver this hygiene awareness and education program will be scoped.
4. How will the project ensure the participation of beneficiaries and affected people, particularly the poor and vulnerable and/or CSOs, during project design to address these issues? Describe the key features, responsibilities, and resources to ensure adequate participation of the poor, excluded and vulnerable groups, and/or CSOs during the project design (may include reference to the TOR for the transaction TA social development specialist or other resources allocated to ensure the participation of the poor, excluded and vulnerable groups, and/or CSOs in the design). CSOs representing the beneficiaries will be consulted or requested to collaborate in the project design include churches and church groups, Development Services Exchange, Solomon Islands National Council of Women, and the Solomon Islands Chamber of Commerce and Industries.
5. What level of CSO participation is planned during the project design? H Information generation and sharing   H Consultation   L Collaboration   NA Partnership Indicate the depth of participation by CSOs in project design by marking high (H), medium (M), low (L), or not applicable (NA) based on the definitions in the table in the Staff Instruction on Promotion of Engagement with Civil Society Organizations.

Note: Text in red is the guidance in the template. Text in blue is a sample response.
Source: Adapted from ADB. Solomon Islands Urban Water Supply and Sanitation Sector Project. Initial poverty and social analysis.

Table 3: Forms and Levels of Stakeholder Participation – Collaboration

Approach	Definitions	Project Processing	Project Implementation
Collaboration (Depth: Low, Medium, or High)	CSOs and ADB/ recipient/client work jointly, but CSOs have limited control over decision-making and resources.	**Low:** Inputs from specific CSOs sought in project design **Medium:** Significant CSO representation on project design body **High:** CSO influence on project design body and agreement of role for CSOs in project implementation	**Low:** CSO input in monitoring and evaluation **Medium:** Stakeholder organization (e.g., CSO) implementation of a project component **High:** Significant CSO representation on project implementation body and participation in implementation activities

ADB = Asian Development Bank, CSO = civil society organization.
Source: ADB. 2012. *Strengthening Participation for Development Results: An Asian Development Bank Guide to Participation.* Manila.

Further guidance is available in *Strengthening Participation for Development Results: An Asian Development Bank Guide to Participation*.

Japan Fund for Prosperous and Resilient Asia and the Pacific
Typical Japan Fund for Prosperous and Resilient Asia and the Pacific (JFPR) activities include support for the development of CSO activities targeting poverty reduction and social development. JFPR-financed projects must be designed using participatory approaches working with the recipients in the DMC, including CSOs. OM E2 describes the business processes for a JFPR-financed project.

Japan established the fund in May 2000 to provide grants for projects supporting poverty reduction and related social development activities that can add value to projects financed by ADB. In 2010, the fund expanded its scope of grant assistance to provide TA grants in addition to project grants. Priority is placed on the poorest and most vulnerable groups living in destitution in ADB DMCs, primarily on innovative programs designed or implemented by local communities or NGOs which contribute to the achievement of the Sustainable Development Goals (SDGs).[49] An example of a JFPR-financed project is in Box 13.

BOX 13

The scale of the COVID-19 pandemic and the impacts of widespread restrictions on movement to contain the virus required a community-based response. CSOs, through their networks of community groups and their understanding of the assets and resources available in their communities, are well-placed to respond to these needs promptly. The services of many existing community social welfare programs—such as food and meal delivery schemes, care services to vulnerable individuals and households, and information and helpline services—have been in higher demand during the pandemic. To support such work, for example, ADB committed $2 million in cofinancing from the Japan Fund for Prosperous and Resilient Asia and the Pacific for TA to help CSOs respond to needs arising from COVID-19. The project, Mitigating the Impact of COVID-19 through Community-Led Interventions, will help CSOs provide services for community-based activities to mitigate and prevent COVID-19; social protection for vulnerable communities, including older person care; and economic support for those whose livelihoods are affected by the pandemic.[a]

ADB = Asian Development Bank, COVID-19 = coronavirus disease, CSO = civil society organization, TA = technical assistance.
[a] ADB. Regional: Mitigating the Impact of COVID-19 through Community-Led Interventions.
Source: Asian Development Bank.

Designing a project that incorporates civil society organization engagement
ADB is committed to working with CSOs throughout the project cycle, particularly drawing on their expertise in participatory and grassroots approaches, leveraging their skills in engaging with poor and vulnerable groups, and mobilizing women and youth.[50]

[49] ADB. Funds and Resources. Japan Fund for Poverty Reduction.
[50] Footnote 16.

The involvement of CSOs in implementing projects should be planned at the design stage of the project cycle. Examples of how CSOs may be involved in ADB-financed projects include (i) assisting and reaching communities; (ii) designing and delivering safeguards, gender action plan, and social development action plan outputs; (iii) delivering goods, services, and community works; (iv) monitoring projects; (v) assisting in FCAS and disaster and emergency situations; and (vi) contributing to regional cooperation and integration (RCI).

These roles are described below.

Assisting and reaching communities:
(i)   Representing beneficiaries of ADB-financed projects and providing information on their needs on issues such as urban services, rural livelihoods, transport, energy access, health and education, financial inclusion, and others.
(ii)   Helping ADB and DMC governments reach and mobilize specific vulnerable groups, e.g., women, youth, disabled people, affected people, older persons, and/or groups in communities.
(iii)   Mobilizing communities and facilitating consultations with communities.
(iv)   Communicating with communities such as to disseminate information about projects and their impacts.

Designing and delivering safeguards, gender action plan (GAP), and social development action plan (SDAP) outputs:
(i)   Supporting safeguards, such as with design and implementation of the involuntary resettlement plans, assessment, and monitoring of environmental impacts, and on indigenous people's plans. CSOs may be engaged to monitor environmental safeguards for category A and B projects. Assisting with the design and implementation of grievance redress mechanisms.
(ii)   Supporting gender activities, including design, implementation, and/or monitoring the GAP. Women's CSOs are typically a trusted resource for women and may provide information, services and/or advocacy on women's and girls' issues. Specialist CSOs may focus by age, with young women and girls' interests being supported by CSOs at local, national, and international levels.

Delivering goods, services, and community works:
(i)   Delivering tailored services and programs to vulnerable groups in sectors including health, education, livelihoods, agriculture, financial services, and more.
(ii)   Delivering tailored services related to prevention, mitigation, and response to GBV/SEAH, including awareness raising, monitoring and reporting, referral mechanisms, legal, psychological, and medical support to survivors of GBV/SEAH, provided in a gender-sensitive manner and based on the principles of a "survivor-centered approach."[51]
(iii)   Designing and delivering awareness raising campaigns, sensitization activities, and initiatives where communities need to change behavior such as road safety, HIV/AIDS awareness, environmental campaigns, and public health campaigns.
(iv)   Providing training, capacity building, and mentoring programs such as financial management training for water user groups, training trade apprentices, livelihood restoration training for resettled project-affected persons, youth economic empowerment and start-up or entrepreneurial programs, training for community service providers, and others.

---

[51]   ADB bases its support to survivors on a set of principles of a "survivor-centered approach" and will aim to create a supportive environment in which the survivor's rights and needs are prioritized, and in which the survivor is treated with dignity and respect. It promotes and supports survivor's needs and wishes, as well as reinforces the survivor's capacity to make decisions about possible interventions.

(v)   Conducting research and community-based surveys such as willingness to pay, poverty and social analysis, gender analysis, participatory rapid appraisals, WASH awareness, and others.

(vi)   Constructing small-scale infrastructure such as paths and roads, solar farms, health centers, reconstruction of disaster affected housing, temporary shelter, community irrigation schemes, and others.

(vii)   Procuring goods for project use using local resources such as medical supplies, water purification equipment, and others.

(viii) Monitoring project activities such as procurement, construction activities, storage of supplies, community activities, behavior change, and others.

(ix)   Assisting in fragile, conflict-affected, disaster, and emergency situations such as providing emergency relief, supporting community-based disaster risk management, early recovery activities, and offering community trauma support.

(x)   Contributing to RCI such as design of cross-border transport and logistics agreements, trade facilitation initiatives, including regional food safety frameworks, border area development, and regional tourism collaboration.

BOX 14

ADB's response to the COVID-19 pandemic includes working with UN agencies such as UNICEF and WHO in supporting the COVID-19 vaccination program in the South Asia region. Under the Responsive COVID-19 Vaccines for Recovery (RECOVER) Project in Sri Lanka,[a] local CBOs will be engaged in communicating information to local communities, identification of targeted populations, and in organizing vaccination-related activities for excluded and vulnerable groups, including those from geographically remote and economically disadvantaged areas. In Nepal, the Government of Nepal will work with UNICEF under a TA and work with local CSOs, such as the local Red Cross societies and the local scouts groups, to increase awareness by mobilizing community volunteers from local organizations.[b] At least 3,000 (with at least 30% women) trained community-level volunteers, from organizations like the Red Cross, will be engaged in door-to-door visits to raise awareness on risks of COVID-19 and benefits of vaccination in high-risk municipalities to support outreach work. In India, vulnerable groups' awareness of the benefit of vaccines will increase, through establishing partnerships with rural banking networks, and new types of CSOs as an innovative pathway to reach out to larger numbers of underserved populations. This activity will target at least 20 partners, networks, or platforms to work with most disadvantaged communities.[c]

CBO = community-based organization, COVID-19 = coronavirus disease, CSO = civil society organization, TA = technical assistance, UN = United Nations, WHO = World Health Organization.
[a] ADB. Democratic Socialist Republic of Sri Lanka: Responsive COVID-19 Vaccines for Recovery under the Asia Pacific Vaccine Access Facility.
[b] ADB. Nepal: Portfolio Management and Capacity Development for Enhanced Portfolio Performance.
[c] ADB. India: Supporting COVID-19 Response and Vaccination Program.
Source: Asian Development Bank.

Documenting planned civil society organization engagement in projects

In undertaking the PSA, project teams must bring together the analysis into the summary poverty reduction and social strategy (SPRSS). The SPRSS brings together the PSA across the dimensions of poverty and social, participation and empowering the poor (including CSO engagement), gender and development, safeguards, other social risks, and monitoring and evaluation. The SPRSS is mandatory for the report and recommendation of the President (RRP). In completing SPRSS part II, participation and empowering the poor, staff should articulate the planned CSO engagement during project implementation, if any. Recognizing that the SPRSS is a summary, criteria for procuring CSOs, their roles, and funding allocated for CSO project engagement should clearly be detailed in the RRP and linked documents, particularly the project administration manual (PAM).[52] The SPRSS is the primary document the NGOC uses to determine whether a project has planned, meaningful CSO engagement and, as such, if it should be counted as contributing to ADB's corporate results framework.

In completing SPRSS part II, participation and empowering the poor, staff should articulate the following:

(i) If CSOs will have a role in the project, a summary of the actions planned to ensure their participation.

(ii) How the project ensures adequate participation of CSOs.

(iii) The approaches and depths to participation of CSOs in the project (as outlined in Table 1).

(iv) If any of the participatory approaches listed are planned, meaningful CSO engagement, a project level participation plan is mandatory to ensure adequate participation of CSOs, the poor and vulnerable, including women in the project implementation.[53]

CSO engagement may be incorporated into a stand-alone participation plan or CSO engagement elements may be incorporated into other plans such as SDAP, GAP, or the gender equality and social inclusion plan. These plans must crucially include monitoring indicators and the budget for CSO engagement. A participation plan describes the planned roles of different stakeholder groups in the project, how their engagement will occur, what method will be used and the timelines or budget for the activities. Participation plans are useful to guide the choice of an appropriate participatory methodology and who will be responsible for implementing participatory activities. The template for a participation plan is in Table 4. More information on how to develop a participation plan is in *Strengthening Participation for Development Results: An Asian Development Bank Guide to Participation*, tool 4, developing a participation plan.

Table 4: Participation Plan Template

Stakeholder group	Objective of their Intervention	Approach to Participation and Depth (information generation and sharing, consultation, collaboration, partnership)	Participation Methods (e.g. workshop, participatory appraisal, survey)		Timeline		Cost Estimate
	Why they are Included		Method	Who Will Be Responsible	Start Date	End Date	

Source: Asian Development Bank.

Table 5: Sample Responses for Summary Poverty Reduction and Social Strategy, Part II

---

52 ....
53

II. PARTICIPATION AND EMPOWERING THE POOR[g]
1. Participatory approaches and project activities that will strengthen inclusiveness in project implementation. Summarize the participatory approaches and the planned project activities that will strengthen inclusiveness and empower the poor and vulnerable[h] and excluded groups during project implementation.[i] Explain how these are reflected in the DMF, GAP, safeguards documents, SDAP, loan agreement, and the PAM. Extensive consultations with national and regional government, VET managers, teachers and students, CSOs and

Table 6: Forms and Levels of Stakeholder Participation – Collaboration

Approach	Definitions	Project Processing	Project Implementation
Collaboration (Depth: Low, Medium, or High)	CSOs and ADB/recipient/client work jointly, but CSOs have limited control over decision-making and resources.	**Low:** Inputs from specific CSOs sought in project design **Medium:** Significant CSO representation on project design body	**Low:** CSO input in monitoring and evaluation **Medium:** Stakeholder organization (e.g., CSO) implementation of a project component
		High: CSO influence on project design body and agreement of role for CSOs in project implementation	**High:** Significant CSO representation on project implementation body and participation in implementation activities

Source: ADB. 2012. *Strengthening Participation for Development Results: An Asian Development Bank Guide to Participation*. Manila.

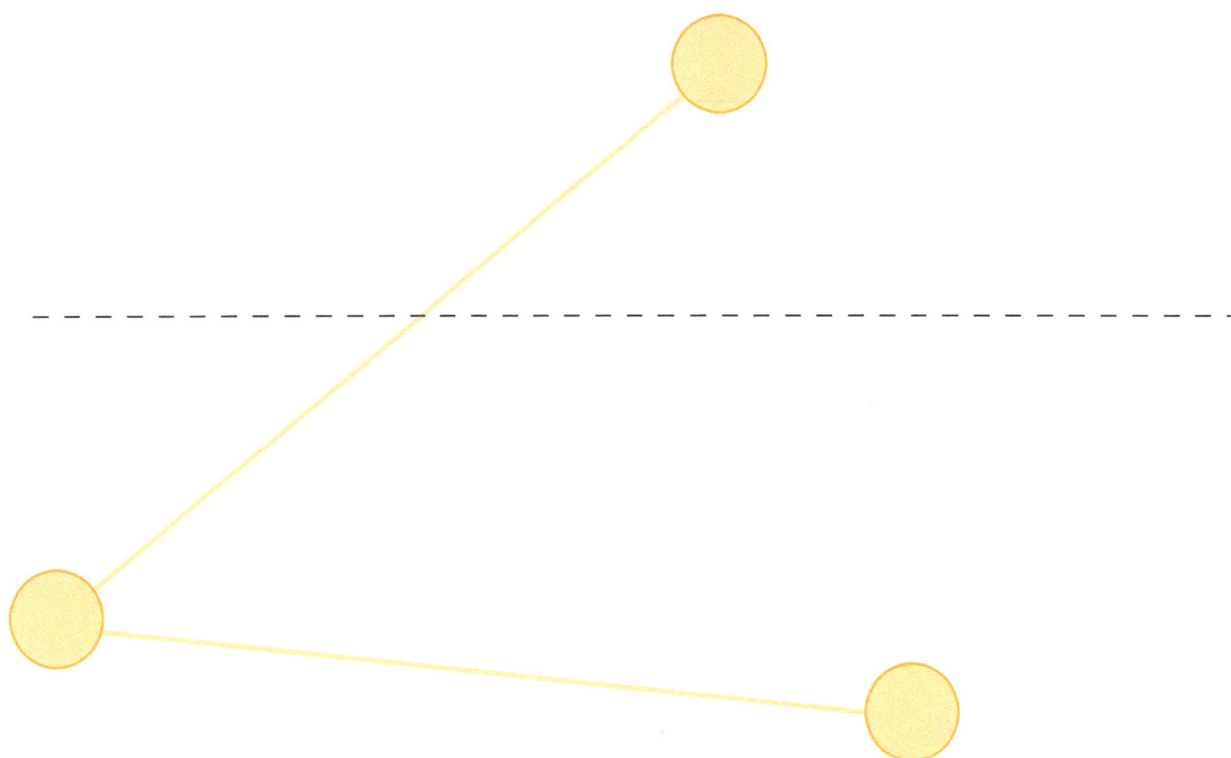

If the SPRSS indicates a high level of information generation and sharing, and/or a high level of consultation and/or any level of collaboration and/or partnership as defined in Table 1, the project will be tagged as having planned, meaningful CSO engagement. ADB will report if this planned, meaningful CSO engagement has been delivered in the corporate results framework in the year that the PCR is circulated to the Board. The SPRSS rating for the approach and depth of participation will be verified through other documents in the RRP such as the design and monitoring framework (DMF), GAP, safeguards document, stakeholder communication strategy, and the project PAM. If a project is determined to have planned, meaningful civil society organization engagement, then the project officer will report in the PCR whether the planned CSO engagement was delivered or not.

See later in this section for further information on ADB's CSO indicator under ADB's corporate results framework.

CSO engagement should also be documented in the SPRSS for policy-based loans and results-based loans. Under most policy-based and results-based loans, the opportunities for CSO engagement within the loan or grant implementation period may be limited, as the loan or grant is paid upon the satisfactory achievement of the identified policy actions or results. However, there may be opportunities for government–CSO engagement within the policy actions, and these should be recorded in the SPRSS.

Further guidance on developing a participation plan is available in *Strengthening Participation for Development Results: An Asian Development Bank Guide to Participation.*[54]

Civil society organization engagement under knowledge and support technical assistance

A knowledge and support TA may be sovereign or nonsovereign. It can also be regional or covering a stand-alone TA for one DMC or a regional TA covering more than one DMC.

Although most projects that formally engage with CSOs use ADB's standard procurement procedures or partnership approaches, ADB projects have engaged CSOs in a number of other effective and meaningful ways through knowledge and support TA, including pilot testing project approaches, transfer of funds, and knowledge partnerships. The Procurement Policy does not cover all such approaches. However, when a legal agreement, including specific guidance is in place, staff can utilize these approaches. Where use of public funds is considered, the financing (including grants) must demonstrate that the funds are used as agreed on in the legal instrument governing their use.[55]

CSOs may also be engaged as knowledge partners.

Implementing and monitoring a project with civil society organization engagement

Like all ADB-financed projects, a project with CSO engagement is implemented in line with its project documents, including the project administration manual. Changes to planned CSO engagement, particularly on projects with planned, meaningful CSO engagement, should be documented in the aide-mémoire, memoranda of understanding, back-to-office reports, midterm reviews, or other monitoring documents. Business processes for changes in scope in loan projects are in PAI 5.02.[56]

---

[54] Footnote 19.

[55] This is detailed in OM J7 operational procedures para. 9, which includes the following ADB auditing requirements: (ii) specific additional auditor's opinion(s) on whether (a) the proceeds of the loan were used only for the purpose(s) of the project. ADB. 2015. Project Financial Reporting and Auditing. *Operations Manual.* OM J7. Manila.

[56] ADB. 2018. Change in Loan Projects. *Project Administration Instructions.* PAI 5.02. Manila.

On sovereign projects, the ADB project team leader will do a review mission twice a year, and usually once a year (depending on the potential risks associated with the projects) for nonsovereign operations, to assess project progress. During these review missions, team leaders should review the performance of CSO consultants, as appropriate. During these missions, ADB includes the capacity development needs of the CSO and how effective their working relations are with the executing and implementing agencies and ADB project staff. The project teams should make recommendations for improvement or changes, if needed.

CSOs must submit regular progress reports and a project completion report to the project management unit (PMU) of the executing and implementing agency and the ADB project team leader in line with its contract, just as any other consulting firm is required to.

Roles for civil society organizations in monitoring projects

ADB and DMCs may engage CSOs to help promote governance, improve accountability, and enhance anticorruption efforts in ADB-financed projects. CSOs may be engaged under ADB-financed projects as consulting firms or service providers to perform safeguards monitoring activities. In high-risk contexts, such as FCAS or highly complex projects, ADB may engage CSOs directly to provide third-party monitoring services to monitor the preparation and/or implementation of safeguards mitigation plans. The borrower or client can also engage qualified CSOs to provide external safeguards monitoring services for projects with significant safeguards impacts.

CSO monitoring of ADB-financed projects enhances governance and accountability and promotes anticorruption efforts. Where possible, dependent on the CSO capacity and at the government's request, staff should make efforts to enable CSOs to monitor governance and anticorruption aspects of projects during implementation. CSO monitoring is particularly important in high-profile loans, such as ADB's COVID-19 Policy Response Options (for further discussion on CSO roles in monitoring large COVID-19 response loans, see Box 4). CSO monitoring is designed to meet ADB's commitment under ADB's Second Governance and Anticorruption Action Plan to involve CSOs in project oversight and promote links between DMC governments and their citizens.[57]

At a DMC's request, CSOs may be engaged to monitor aspects of an ADB-financed project, such as GAP implementation or results-based program lending. CSOs may be engaged for external verification of disbursement-linked indicators, as they are independent of government, including executing and implementing agencies.[58] In all these cases, CSOs would be engaged as consulting firms or service providers.

CSOs may also independently monitor ADB-financed projects, without being requested or procured to do so by ADB or the government. Advocacy groups, particularly those with a mandate in monitoring public expenditure, transparency, and anticorruption, may monitor ADB-financed projects for accountability and transparency purposes. Advocacy organizations may have valuable information about project or policy implementation that is otherwise unavailable to ADB or the government, which should be considered. When such information relates to concerns, ADB and the DMC government should proactively follow up such information to understand and address the issues, as appropriate.

Grassroots organizations should be engaged to monitor ADB-financed projects, wherever this is feasible.[59]

---

[57] Footnote 24.
[58] ADB. 2019. *Mainstreaming the Results-Based Lending for Programs.* Manila.
[59] Footnote 41.

Further guidance on participatory monitoring is available in *Strengthening Participation for Development Results: An Asian Development Bank Guide to Participation*[60] (tool 7 participatory monitoring and evaluation) and *Participation Tools for the Pacific – Part 6 Monitoring and Evaluation.*[61]

Project completion and closing a project using civil society organization engagement

CSOs can be engaged as consultants or service providers on ADB-financed projects as an independent evaluator or monitor, independent of government, the private sector, and ADB. Irrespective of whether a CSO is engaged as an evaluator, governments are responsible for conducting project evaluations; ADB project teams are responsible for self-evaluation; and the Independent Evaluation Department is responsible for independent evaluation.

PAI 6.07A details the instructions for completing PCRs for sovereign operations, while PAI 6.07B details the instructions for completing Extended Annual Review Reports for nonsovereign operations.[62]

Tracking Project-Level Civil Society Organization Engagement in ADB Operations

The NGOC tracks CSO participation in ADB-financed operations. ADB reports its performance against its planned CSO engagement in ADB's annual Development Effectiveness Review. ADB measures actual completed CSO participation, as reported in the project completion report, against planned CSO participation, as documented in the SPRSS.[63] The NGOC reviews the projects that circulate a PCR to the Board in a given year to determine which had planned, meaningful CSO engagement and to see if the PCR indicates that planned CSO engagement took place. The NGOC reports the number that delivered as a percentage of those that had planned, meaningful CSO engagement.[64] If the PCR indicates that the planned, meaningful CSO engagement took place, the project is counted as having delivered CSO engagement. It is, therefore, counted as having fulfilled the CSO engagement requirement for the purposes of the corporate results framework indicator.

ADB measures actual completed CSO participation as reported in the PCR, against planned CSO participation as documented in the SPRSS, and other documents as part of loan or grant approval. Annually, the NGOC will review the projects which have PCRs published that year. ADB will only review projects which had planned, meaningful CSO engagement in sovereign projects.

For the purposes of the corporate results framework indicator, ADB draws its definition of meaningful CSO engagement from the approaches and depths of participation in Table 1. Projects classified as planning meaningful CSO engagement are those which exhibit these types of participation with corresponding depths:
- (i)   Information Generation and Sharing: High
- (ii)   Consultation: High

---

[60] ADB. 2012. *Strengthening Participation for Development Results: An Asian Development Bank Guide to Participation.* Manila.

[61] L.C. Thomas et al. 2019. Participation Tools for the Pacific – Part 6 Monitoring and Evaluation. Development Asia. Manila.

[62] ADB. 2019. Project Completion Report for Sovereign Operations. *Project Administration Instructions.* PAI 6.07A. Manila; ADB. 2018. Extended Annual Review Reports for Nonsovereign Operations. *Project Administration Instructions.* PAI 6.07B. Manila.

[63] While the SPRSS is the preferred source of information on planned, meaningful CSO engagement, the following can also be used to verify planned, meaningful CSO engagement: (i) RRP, (ii) DMF, (iii) GAP or gender equality and social inclusion action plans, (iv) safeguards documents, (v) stakeholder communication strategy, and (vi) the project administration manual.

[64] Meaningful CSO engagement is defined as having the following types of participation with corresponding depths indicated in the SPRSS: high information generation and sharing; high consultation; or any level of collaboration or partnership (Table 1 provides more details on the definitions of each level).

(iii)   Collaboration: Low, medium, or high
(iv)   Partnership: Low, medium, or high

Recording the civil society organization engagement in the project completion report

Staff and DMC officials should record any CSO engagement that took place during the project's implementation. If there was planned, meaningful CSO engagement, as detailed in the RRP, SPRSS, or other linked documents to the RRP,[65] then staff should report in the PCR if the planned activities took place. PAI 6.07A details the instructions for completing PCRs for sovereign operations.[66]

Questions and answers on the CSO indicator under ADB's corporate results framework

Q   **What other sources may be considered in assessing planned CSO engagement?**
While the SPRSS is the preferred source of information on planned CSO engagement, these documents may also verify planned CSO engagement:
(i)   report and recommendation of the President,
(ii)   design and monitoring framework,
(iii)   gender action plan,
(iv)   safeguards documents, and
(v)   project administration manual, including the stakeholder communications strategy.

Q   **Which projects will be evaluated under the new indicator?**
All projects that have a PCR circulated in a given year will be included in the rating.

Q   **Can we include projects which did not have planned CSO engagement, but had meaningful CSO engagement during implementation?**
Unfortunately, no. The indicator only reports how ADB has delivered what it planned. Notwithstanding, this CSO engagement could be captured in other ways, such as case studies in annual reports on ADB–CSO cooperation.

Q   **How do we account for projects with two (or more) types of planned CSO engagement, but only one took place?**
If the CSO engagement which took place is deemed meaningful, then it counts as having fulfilled its planned CSO engagement.

---

[65]   Footnote 63.
[66]   ADB. 2019. Project Completion Report for Sovereign Operations. *Project Administration Instructions*. PAI 6.07A. Manila.

Q **I am fielding a midterm review soon. What are the implications of the revised indicator on my mission?**

Midterm review mission teams are strongly encouraged to document and take stock of the progress on planned CSO engagement, so that this can be appropriately reflected in the PCR.

Q **When did the revised indicator come into effect?**

ADB's *2021 Development Effectiveness Report,* which reported on 2020, was the first time ADB used the revised indicator to report on CSO engagement.

3

Consultations with Civil Society Organizations

Principles for Effective Consultations with Civil Society Organizations

Staff and developing member country (DMC) officials responsible for designing, implementing, and monitoring Asian Development Bank (ADB) operations should consider the following principles and tips for organizing effective consultations with civil society organizations (CSOs).

Some key concepts to consider

Definition of consultation. An event whereby stakeholder input is requested and considered as part of an inclusive policy, program, or project decision-making process. A consultation seeks inputs, ideas, and feedback. Carefully targeted engagement may be needed for marginalized groups. ADB's publication on *Strengthening Participation For Development Results: An Asian Development Bank Guide To Participation* is a useful resource.[67]

What consultations are not. Consultations are not presentations about a project or initiative with a question and answer (Q&A) session, explanations of how, for example, resettlement will take place, or other information sharing meetings. Consultations are not public relations exercises, although they do build good will.

What are the benefits of consultation. Consultations build ownership of the project among partners and beneficiaries, they provide useful information on issues that the government or other stakeholders may not provide, they reduce the likelihood of complaints or other concerns being raised later and, most importantly, they contribute to improving project design and implementation.

Consult with civil society organizations during policy development and review. Staff should conduct meaningful consultations with CSOs during policy development or review, country partnership strategy (CPS) preparation, and as part of the project preparation due diligence process. Team leaders are responsible for ensuring that consultations meet good practice standards for the context. Consultations are an ongoing process and not a single event.

Consult with civil society organizations during project design phase. Engaging with CSOs at the design phase will give staff an understanding of their expertise, capacity, and capability. Speak to CSOs and conduct informal capacity assessments to find out their capacities and constraints and incorporate capacity-building as a necessary precondition of CSO engagement. This will assist staff in designing a project that has meaningful CSO engagement and the necessary support and capacity-building to skill up the CSOs to be "ADB-ready."

---

[67] Footnote 19.

Before the consultation

Design the consultation. Successful consultations start with a participatory design that is in itself a product of consultation. Some countries have a wider range of stakeholders than others. Therefore, it can be useful to have a pre-consultation meeting with a local CSO to learn about the local context or the consultation methodology in advance of the consultation.

Set a clear objective for the consultation. Determine the specific reason for the consultation and be clear on the influence the consultations will have. Determine targets for participation of different groups (i.e., women, girls, people with a disability, boys, young men, and others), as appropriate. Ensure that participants' expectations for the consultations are in line with the consultation objective. If focus questions are to be used to draw out inputs, frame the questions during the design phase consultations with CSOs. Based on the objectives and focus questions, it will also help to determine the appropriateness of the consultation methods, participants, language, timing, and location. Some questions that must be answered include the following:

(i)   Is it appropriate to have men and women in the same consultation?

(ii)   Are there sensitivities around different ethnic or religious groups? Or age groups? Or gender orientation and sexual identity?

(iii)   Will participants be comfortable speaking if there are other stakeholder groups present? Some advocacy groups recommend that multistakeholder consultations for community consultation may not be advisable, if pre-consultation discussions indicate that local people are not comfortable in such situations. In other situations, consultations with CSOs are good opportunities for other stakeholders to hear different perspectives. Explore options for having other stakeholder groups participate as observers and agree on ground rules in advance of the consultation.

(iv)   What time of day and location is best to make sure the target participants can participate? Consider, in particular, the unpaid work that women and girls do and its time commitments, or the hours of study for young people. Consider that if women must attend with small children or babies, it is likely to be distracting?

(v)   What language will the participants use? Some participants may not be comfortable using the national language(s) and some may not be literate. Consider if language consultants or interpreters are required.

(vi)   If young people below 18 are involved, have the necessary permissions, especially from parents or guardians, been secured?

(vii)   Consider the methodology (e.g., small group work or focus group discussions, using same or similar age consultants to lead elders, adults, youth, and others) and how to make it useful for the project (e.g., number of people attending, the range of views represented).

(viii) What technology and platforms are best suited to the locale and context? If online consultation will be conducted, what are the considerations for addressing the digital divide? Do data packages need to be provided? Remember that some participants do not have easy access to digital devices and may need to use an internet café or friend's device. Think through the safety and security issues surrounding this.

(ix)   How can the consultation be advertised so that people will come? How long does it need to be advertised for, and where is this best place to advertise so that the target groups are aware of it?

(x)   Consider ethical and safety issues. Are safety and health protocols needed for face-to-face interactions? If so, what are the requirements? Are there other safety and ethical considerations that need to be taken when consultations require the participation of specific groups (survivors of gender-based violence, persons with disabilities, LGBT+, and others)? Have confidentiality and disclosure considerations been considered and explained? Has a complaints mechanism, for complaints about the consultation process, been established and provided to participants?

Adopt an inclusive approach. Adopt an inclusive approach to the design and implementation of projects and tap the potential and expertise of CSOs to advise on inclusive approaches. Determine how the consultation will ensure the voice of all vulnerable groups is heard and determine what level of their participation is a target for meetings. Engage with a range of CSOs. Appreciate the diversity of CSOs. Do not assume that communities are homogenous and are able to be represented by one CSO. Engaging a range of CSOs and community-based organizations (CBOs) recognizes the heterogenous nature of communities. Different CSOs and CBOs may cater to different subgroups such as women, youth, and minority groups. Additionally, there may be different groups within these subgroups (such as those based around linguistic or ethnic groupings). Measures to protect the well-being of vulnerable groups should be incorporated (e.g., if working with children and youth). There are CSOs that specialize in these methodologies. Ensure that the consultation space is a "safe space" and that CSOs are free to express opinion without fear. Be sure to broaden CSO engagement out of urban areas to peri-urban, regional, and remote CSOs. Not all CSOs will have the same views, and some may have opposing views to other CSOs. Ensure that resources are allocated for inclusive participation.

Pay close attention to gender and social inclusion. Consider also how people with hearing-, sight-, other physical disability or cognitive-impairment, especially women and girls in this sector, may participate in consultations on ADB-financed projects or policy. Consideration needs to be given to how these groups may travel to consultations, and what additional support is required to allow inclusive participation. Consider whether women-only teams are preferable, according to the context, and be aware of cultural and social sensitivities about female teams' travel. How will the voices of young people and children, the aged and infirm, the marginalized and excluded, be heard?

Share consultation plans with relevant stakeholders. DMC governments and ADB staff should ensure that both understand the purpose of conducting CSO consultations and the tailored approach that may be undertaken in each DMC. Government officials need to ensure that ADB staff are apprised of the relationship that they may have with CSOs in their DMC, and how consultations need to be tailored to align with existing processes. Similarly, ADB staff need to ensure government clients understand how ADB consults with CSOs and the value that it will bring to project design and development results. Both should work together to develop a consultation plan that aligns with international good practice to improve consultation design.

Organize the consultation team. The consultation team usually consists of a lead facilitator, cofacilitators, documenters, and an information and communication technology (ICT) assistant (if relevant). Engaging a seasoned facilitator, familiar with the sector and the CSO participants, to lead the process is recommended. The ideal facilitator is someone with experience who speaks the local language and understands local culture and political sensitivities, as well as how ADB works. The cofacilitators may be a mix of project staff or members of a CSO. If online consultations are to be conducted, an ICT assistant will be of great help to

BOX 15

Engaging with CSOs during the pandemic involves some special considerations for consultations. It is important to recognize that the COVID-19 pandemic has had a dramatic impact on CSOs' operations. One study from Europe indicates that 64.5% of CSOs reported that the pandemic was having a devastating impact on the sustainability of CSOs, with a "leapfrog" shift to telework that many CSOs were unprepared for. The study indicated that throughout the pandemic, some CSOs had poor digital literacy, limited infrastructure, and faced a reduction in donations. This was coupled with a rise in demand for CSOs' services.[a]

ADB staff and DMC officials need to take these considerations into account when engaging with CSOs.

Some tips for CSO engagement during pandemic conditions include the following:

(i) Provide capacity support for CSOs to support digital literacy and access to online consultations—this could be as practical as providing access to computers and a stable internet connection at the resident mission or government office (if physically open) through to providing financing for training in digital skills audit and training, and upgrading of CSO equipment and infrastructure.

(ii) Do not assume that CSOs can access online consultations—provide a variety of means of notification about the consultation, including mail and hard copy notices in communities, and a variety of ways that CSOs may respond to consultation questions if they are unable to attend online, such as through postal services, telephone, and community suggestion boxes.

(iii) Seek to develop and encourage twinning arrangements between established and well-resourced CSOs, with less well-resourced grassroots CBOs, to support access to technology—twinning arrangements could offer support in digital access for consultations and provides the added benefit of local CBOs working with other more established CSOs, which may act as a catalyst for capacity development.

(iv) Seek engagement with private sector technology operators on how they can support digital engagement with CSOs—many private sector operators have corporate social responsibility pledges and some have programs to support local organizations with digital access.

ADB = Asian Development Bank, CBO = community-based organization, COVID-19 = coronavirus disease, CSO = civil society organization, DMC = developing member country.
[a] European Union, European Economic and Social Committee. 2021. *The response of civil society organizations to face the COVID-19 pandemic and the consequent restrictive measures adopted in Europe*. Brussels.
Source: Asian Development Bank.

ensure connectivity and access to online platforms. Professional documenters will provide comprehensive documentation that is critical in completing the report after the consultation. Ensure that the team advises the CSO participants of the project lead or supervisor, and that this is shared with the CSOs, so that if there are issues or concerns about the way the consultations are conducted, the CSO participants know who to contact about this.

Determine budgetary and logistical requirements. Plan logistics carefully. Consider the time of day and location so it does not prevent the target group (or a part of the target group, i.e., field workers, women) from attending. Is childcare or catering needed? In some communities, catering is expected, and people will not attend unless they know it will be provided: remember that some participants may walk for many hours to attend. For online consultations, consider offering voucher allowances for catering or childcare needs. Consider what technology and platforms are most suitable if consultations are online and be familiar with their use. Agree on the meeting's ground rules and let participants know in advance what these will be. Determine how many people are needed for the most meaningful two-way consultation, and at what size the meeting becomes too big or small to be effective. Share background materials, in the culturally- and age-appropriate format, in advance of the meeting. Have a contingency plan and share it with CSOs in case the meeting cannot go ahead (due to the rainy season or other disruption).

Utilize technology when appropriate. Online consultations can enable ADB to reach more people, although it has constraints as well. Some participants may not be able to engage through online means. Consider what technology is most suitable—what platform(s) is/are most familiar to the participants? Given the ease of recording, ensure that participants consent to the consultation being recorded and clarify who will have access to the recording. Set clear ground rules for how participants will be entitled to time to speak, how questions and answers will be handled, and how privacy and safeguarding will be addressed.

During the consultation

Opening the consultation. It is important to set the mood of each consultation by putting the participants at ease. Participants should know the objectives of the consultation and the expected outputs at the very start. Agree on the meeting's ground rules. Research ethics also recommends that permission should be sought from the participants if voice or video recording is to be made. It is also good practice to prepare age- and sex-disaggregated roster of participants as evidence and to ensure that participants are properly listed and acknowledged in the consultation report. Ensure that participants know they can leave at any time, and can provide feedback at a later stage via a mechanism to solicit contributions from those CSOs who could not attend (as outlined below).

However, consider privacy issues. Consultations may be sensitive events for some CSOs, including some advocacy organizations, some highly vulnerable groups, including LGBT+ people, those at risk of gender-based violence (GBV), and human rights defenders. Consider if and how they will agree for the event to be documented, including in naming the consultation's participants. Likewise, ensure safeguarding young people who participate in consultations in line with international good practice.

Listen. During the consultation, do as much listening as possible, and ensure the environment allows for careful and considered listening. Limit speaking to clarify points, but do not get defensive about issues that arise. Ensure that the consultation is well moderated and that a few people do not dominate the discussion.

Document the consultation. A flip chart is good, as people can see how points are being recorded and can request corrections if necessary. Depending on the issue and the audience, ADB sometimes makes records of consultations public on the ADB website. A local CSO could also be asked to distribute typed or printed minutes to participants after the consultation.

Set up a mechanism to solicit contributions. The CSOs who were not able to attend consultations should be solicited to illustrate to the interested parties that ADB is reaching out. A local CSO could offer to collect written inputs; so too could a local chief or other neutral representative. These should be included in the documentation of the consultation.

Closing the consultation. Explain to the participants how their contributions were used either through a written document or a short follow-up meeting. Inform the participants about the mechanism to solicit more contributions. Earnestly thank the participants and the hosts of the consultation.

Evaluate the consultation. Survey participants to assess how many felt that their inputs were adequately incorporated. How many understood the purpose of the consultation and reason for it? Understanding the value and effectiveness of the consultation to the community is valuable for planning a successful subsequent consultation. Ensure the feedback is incorporated into subsequent consultations to build trust with stakeholders.

After the consultation

Prepare the report. The report contains the processes and outputs of the consultation. This is usually referenced by the documentation of the consultation.

Close the feedback loop. If consulting with CSOs during the design phase, be clear on how the information from the consultations will be used and how it will—or will not—be incorporated into project design or policy review. Give information on the process and expected timelines. Return to CSOs that took the time to consult with you and let them know what happened and what the next steps will be.

Some useful tips

Promote CSO participation. Before the consultations or during the consultation design phase, prepare knowledge products on engagement with CSOs, including details on how this was achieved and the outcomes of the engagement. Invite CSOs to thematic meetings. Highlight the advantages of CSO engagement through blogs, photo essays, and stories of change.

Plan the engagement early. Undertake research on active CSOs in the sector in the DMC and ask government, ADB staff, and consultants about reputable CSOs working in the project sector. Seek CSO anchor and NGO and Civil Society Center (NGOC) advice on which CSOs are active in the sector and DMC or region of interest. Undertake a stakeholder analysis to identify key CSOs and their motivations, interests, and constraints. Consider convening a pre-consultation meeting with CSO representatives to learn more about the local context and CSO capacity. In some communities, it is important to seek permission to engage.

Inform the target audience early. Consider how and when you will inform the target audience about the consultation. Participants should be prepared for a consultation, as they will make more informed, thought-out contributions. Good practice is to announce the consultation at least 2 weeks in advance, with a clear consultation objective and agenda. Determine how to advertise so the target group will know about it. Relying on e-mail is not appropriate in some communities, as some people may not have computer or internet access or may have limited electricity supply. In such situations, consider letters, flyers, or announcements after other community meetings to advertise to the target audience. In other situations, social media may be the most effective approach to reaching participants.

✓ **Use engagement materials and processes that are culturally sensitive**. Ensure that materials are in the language and dialect of the region. Research if heavily text-based material, or more visual or shorter materials, are the appropriate form of communication with community-based CSOs. Use respected local facilitators with local knowledge to assist with CSO engagement. Be prepared to hold separate consultations with women or marginalized groups. Understand local customs and norms, particularly gender, ethnic, identity, religious, and age-based mores, including a potential reluctance to speak if those in authority are present, women may be reluctant to speak in front of men, youth deferring to community elders, and other customs.

4

Due Diligence, Procurement, and Partnerships

Identifying and Assessing the Capacity of Civil Society Organizations

Identifying suitable civil society organizations

The following ADB resources offer useful tools for assisting in identifying suitable civil society organizations (CSOs):

(i)   Refer to the stakeholder analysis prepared during the country partnership strategy (CPS). The stakeholder analysis should be a "living" document that is regularly updated and refreshed as more information on stakeholders, particularly CSOs, is gathered.

(ii)   CSO anchors in the resident mission who are familiar with CSOs operating in the country and have contacts with apex organizations. See NGO and Civil Society Contacts for a list of CSO anchors.

(iii)   ADB's Civil Society Briefs on developing member countries (DMCs). These briefs contain a list of some of the larger, well-established CSOs.

(iv)   ADB's consultant management system (CMS) allows firms to categorize themselves as CSOs. ADB staff and project management units (PMUs) can search the CMS database to see which CSOs are registered in a country or with a specific country or sector expertise.

(v)   ADB staff and DMC officials can ask for information from CSO umbrella organizations, which are also listed in ADB's Civil Society Briefs. An internet search can also help identify these groups, which may focus on a country or a sector within a country.

(vi)   CSO anchors in resident missions may present potential projects based on the country programming documents that could use CSO competencies, and request interested organizations to attend.

ADB staff and DMC officials may search and identify CSOs with the expertise needed for a specific loan, grant or technical assistance (TA) project and invite them to apply.[68] Be sure to first check ADB's sanctions list.

CSO link database. The ADB contacts database is an internal repository of contacts. Contact the NGO and Civil Society Center (NGOC) for further information.

Assessing the capacity of civil society organizations

Prototype questionnaires have been formulated for assessing potential CSO partners that can help determine whether a particular CSO is appropriate to work on an ADB-financed project. The questionnaires typically cover the following organizational aspects or assessment areas of CSO capacity: (i) legal status, (ii) credibility, (iii) mission and governance, (iv) constituency and support, (v) technical capacity, (vi) managerial capacity, (vii) administrative capacity, and (viii) financial capacity.

An example questionnaire is provided in Appendix 5.

---

[68]   Integrity due diligence should be undertaken on the proposed or nominated CSO before engagement, in accordance with the applicable ADB rules, instructions, and guidelines. ADB's Office of Anticorruption and Integrity should be consulted on the scope of integrity due diligence.

While such prototype questionnaires provide valuable insights into the CSO selection and assessment process, it is not a one-size-fits-all tool for assessing a potential CSO. Neither does there exist a particular "passing grade" for the completed questionnaire. Instead, DMC officials and ADB project officers themselves must judge based on the planned engagement, whether or not the responses to the questionnaire provide sufficient confidence that the CSO will be suitable. Ultimately, the question that must be answered is whether the CSO under consideration is able to fulfill the responsibilities required of it under the particular ADB-financed activity.

An important point to note is that ADB and DMC governments require the services of CSOs that are proven and reliable in the tasks relevant to their contributions to the project, not necessarily in all aspects of the project. For example, for a project on microfinance support, the relevant CSOs may be needed for their strengths in community outreach and entrepreneurship or livelihoods development and training, but they would not be required to be experts in microfinance policy, banking systems, and capital raising.

Additionally, those CSOs with specific identified weaknesses in administration or finance systems may be suitable if part of the terms of reference (TOR) requires the CSOs to engage a dedicated finance or administration officer with experience in ADB-financed projects. DMC officials and ADB staff can also build in capacity support to the project activities to assist such CSOs.

Important note for assessing CSOs—when CSOs are not genuine. Some CSOs may falsely claim to represent populations—often vulnerable people—who have not agreed to, or are not even aware of, claims to such representation. Some CSOs many purport to represent particular groups, e.g., landowners, community members, vulnerable groups, but have no such mandate from these groups. In addition, while most CSOs are what they present themselves to be, a small proportion are not genuine CSOs. These include "paper NGOs" or "briefcase nongovernment organizations (NGOs)." They may appear to be a full-scale organizations, but actually exist on paper (or in "a briefcase") only, created for individual profit or employment and, therefore, do not have the capacity, expertise, or local credibility to deliver the expected results. Unfortunately, these organizations may present well and occasionally receive donor funding. The idea of the "briefcase NGO" suggests a slick, business-like operation, but ultimately, some or all of the funds sourced under the name of the paper or briefcase CSO may be diverted to the "founder(s)" or "principal(s)"—above fair salaries and wages.

Staff and DMC officials must conduct thorough due diligence on all CSOs. Items to look for to ensure that the organization is a genuine CSO include an organizational bank account with at least two signatories, registration with the relevant authority, a legal personality, reputable members on its board, reputable staff members (including financial management staff), verifiable examples of past works (within the scope of its mandate), verifiable experience working with the communities which it purports to represent, evaluation reports demonstrating community-based feedback, and links with community-based focal points (who can verify the work of the CSO). Verbal references and testimonials from past funders and community members are another tool to verify a CSO's credentials. Tables 7 and 8 will assist in assessing CSOs' capacity.

Many CSOs are required to undertake capacity assessments for other development partners to qualify for funding and/or as part of networks they have joined. There is also a range of resources available for CSOs to conduct self-assessments. It may be more efficient to ask a CSO to submit a recent capacity assessment, if available, rather than undertaking a new one. Further information on external organizations' capacity assessments for CSOs and self-assessments for CSOs is in Appendix 2. Further guidance on assessing CSOs is available in *Strengthening Participation for Development Results: An Asian Development Bank Guide to Participation* on p. 55.[69]

---

[69]   Footnote 19.

Assessing a CSO for implementing a specific loan, grant or technical assistance project

To ensure that the most qualified CSO is engaged to undertake and implement an activity under an ADB-financed loan, grant or TA project, the project executing and implementing agencies should begin by writing a detailed TOR. The content of the TOR can be drawn from the project administration manual (PAM), report and recommendation of the President (RRP), gender action plan (GAP), social safeguards plans, and the design and monitoring framework (DMF), by identifying potential actions that fit the role of CSOs in each country context. The DMC government may also use the country's financial management system and planning processes as reference for the TOR for ADB-financed projects. When planning to engage CSOs under results-based loans as independent verification agents, when preparing the TOR, draw from the Project Implementation Document, DMF, and reporting arrangements for results-based loans. The TOR then can be the basis for searching CSOs with the expertise needed for a specific loan, grant or TA project and may be invited to apply.

As a minimum, CSOs engaged in any a specific loan, grant or TA project should
- (i) have a CMS account (see ADB Consultant Management System for further information);
- (ii) employ staff who are citizens or nationals of an ADB member country;
- (iii) not be associated with the firm that prepared the design, specifications, or engaged in the preparation of the project or firm that will provide supervision of the works; and
- (iv) not be sanctioned or temporarily suspended by ADB for a violation of its Anticorruption Policy (1998, as amended to date); see ADB's sanctions list.

However, the lack of a CMS account is the most basic limitation for CSO access to engagement with ADB-financed operations. CSO anchors at the country level can start advocating with CSOs to open and establish a CMS account. Engaging in ADB-financed projects can highlight CSOs' inherent advocacies and expertise and establish a firmer presence at the country level.

CSO scoping and assessment. As part of due diligence, scoping of potential CSOs may occur by examining their mandates, interests, areas of activity, and most importantly, readiness to engage with ADB or the DMC government. Table 7 offers guidance to assist project officers in assessing CSOs' capacities prior to engagement, as a form of market scan for CSOs with the capacity to conduct the planned activity. The checklist in Table 7 below should be considered in light of the different country legal requirements, contexts, and conditions relevant to each CSO. For example, in emergency and disaster situations, accommodations may be made appropriate to the context.

Table 7: Checklist for Assessing Capacity of Civil Society Organizations

Criteria	Documentary Evidence	Yes	No	Remarks
1 Evidence of availability of an independent organizational bank account	Certificate from the bank			Required
2 Primary registration e.g., registered articles of incorporation or evidence of registration as a partnership	Registration certificate or listing			Required, but will differ based on local context
3 Secondary registration e.g., tax registration account, business permit, certificate of registration from the government agency mandated to accredit CSOs in the DMC	Registration certificate or listing			
4 List of minimum key personnel with corresponding qualifications to be assigned to the project, including curriculum vitae	Organizational chart of project management team highlighting participation of women			Required
5 Evidence of adequate financial management capacity and function	Financial management capacity questionnaire (examples and guidance are in Appendix 5 and in ADB financial management assessment guidance documents)[a]			
6 CSO's health and safety program (including, as relevant, COVID-19 guidelines or other specific health and safety guidelines)	Program and guidelines			
7 Evidence of experience as a contractor in the implementation of at least one completed project over the last 3 years of the nature and complexity equivalent to the works covered by the TOR	Certificate of completion, notice of award, notice to proceed, and copy of relevant previous contract			If an equivalent experience is not available, projects implemented by the CSO that approximates the requirements of the TOR can be considered.
8 List of ongoing and completed projects similar to the nature and complexity equivalent to the works covered by the TOR	Descriptions of ongoing and completed projects similar to the nature and complexity equivalent to the works covered by the TOR			If there are no similar projects being implemented, ongoing projects implemented by the CSO that approximates the requirements of the TOR can be considered.

COVID-19 = coronavirus disease, CSO = civil society organization, DMC = developing member country, TOR = terms of reference.

[a] ADB. 2015. *Financial Management Technical Guidance Note: Financial Management Assessment.* Manila; ADB. 2009. *Financial Due Diligence: A Methodology Note.* Manila; and ADB. 2014. *Financial Management Technical Guidance Note: Preparing and Presenting Cost Estimates for Projects and Programs Financed by the Asian Development Bank.* Manila.

Risk rating and mitigation. Building on the results of Table 7, as part of the due diligence measures for readiness of CSOs to be engaged on ADB-financed operations, the risk rating matrix in Table 8 may be applied. Immediate and follow-up measures are provided to guide and assist CSOs to expand their capacities to participate as service providers or consultants in ADB-financed operations.

Table 8: Risk Categorization of Civil Society Organizations

Risk Categories	Indicators – Based on the Checklist for Assessing Capacity of CSOs (Table 7)	Immediate Measures	Follow-up Measures
Low	Evidence of all criteria in the checklist. (8/8 Yeses).		CSOs may be encouraged to submit EOIs and submit bids for the specific loan, grant or TA project that matches their interests and capacities.
Moderate	Evidence for criteria 1, 2, 3, 4, 5, 7, and 8 in the checklist. (7/8 Yeses), but no evidence for criteria 6 (health and safety program, including, as relevant, COVID-19 or other specific health and safety guidelines).	Encourage the CSO to formulate a health and safety program, including, as relevant, COVID-19 or other specific health and safety guidelines.	Upon completion of the health and safety program and the COVID-19 or other specific health and safety guideline, as relevant, the CSOs may be encouraged to submit EOIs for a specific loan, grant or TA project that matches their interests and capacities.
Substantial	No evidence for criteria 5 (financial management capacity and function).	Assist the CSO in building its financial management function and capacity and formulate strategies for financial sustainability.	Prioritize CSO in capacity building programs offered, especially those that will build capacities on financial management functions.
High	No evidence for criteria 1, 2, 3, and 5.	Encourage CSO to establish an organizational bank account. Encourage CSO to acquire primary and secondary registrations. Assist or encourage the CSO in building its financial management function and capacity and formulate strategies for financial sustainability.	Orient CSOs about ADB and on the documentary and fiduciary requirements in submitting EOIs and bids.

ADB = Asian Development Bank, COVID-19 = coronavirus disease, CSO = civil society organization, EOI = expression of interest, TA = technical assistance.

Source: Asian Development Bank.

The results of the scoping and assessment using the criteria (Table 7) and risk rating (Table 8) as part of due diligence will assist in designing the procurement processes for ADB-financed operations. It will provide an indication of not only on the available expertise provided by CSOs, but also about the robustness or scarcity of such expertise.

Opportunities for engagement are sent to CMS account holders on a weekly basis through a request for expression of interest and CSOs send expressions of interest (EOIs) for an opportunity under a specific loan, grant or TA project that they are interested to implement. Following the closure of the request for expression of interest, the project executing and implementing agencies may start assessing and selecting short listed CSOs who submitted an EOI.

ADB requires the conduct of financial analysis and evaluation for all sovereign investment projects (whether loan- or grant-financed). The financial proposal from prospective CSOs is, therefore, required and forms part of the submission in the bidding during the procurement stage of a specific loan, grant or TA project. Guidance on the review of financial proposals is included in relevant ADB technical guidance notes.[70] A timebound financial management action plan should also be required of short listed CSOs.

Where the executing agency and/or implementing agency is a public corporation, a private sector corporation, or other nongovernment entity (such as CSOs, in which case they are known as implementing entities, see footnote 34), a financial analysis of historical and projected financial statements is performed to establish their financial capacity to operate and maintain the network of assets and, if required, service the capital.[71] The evidence of experiences and lists of ongoing and completed projects similar to the nature and complexity equivalent to the works covered by the TOR is one way of ensuring that the CSO is capable of implementing a specific loan, grant or TA project, of the same complexity cost or financial requirement.

The criteria and the process of selection through due diligence will minimize completion risk and execution risks such as delay in implementation and the risk that project outputs will not be completed as intended. These risks can be caused by lack of funding, delayed approval, incorrect procurement, nonperforming contractors, delays in securing environmental clearances, or payment of resettlement compensation, and others.[72]

Project executing and implementing agencies can use the reference material on financial analysis in the Financial Analysis and Evaluation: Technical Guidance Note.[73]

All CSOs entrusted with the responsibility of managing ADB funds are required to
- (i) maintain separate financial records for each project and prepare annual project financial statements in accordance with financial reporting standards acceptable to ADB;[74]
- (ii) submit to ADB audited CSO financial statements annually (fiscal year) until the project closing date;[75] and
- (iii) all other requirements as outlined in Operations Manual section J7 Project Financial Reporting and Auditing.

---

[70] ADB. 2015. *Financial Management Technical Guidance Note: Financial Management Assessment.* Manila; ADB. 2009. *Financial Due Diligence: A Methodology Note.* Manila; and ADB. 2014. *Financial Management Technical Guidance Note: Preparing and Presenting Cost Estimates for Projects and Programs Financed by the Asian Development Bank.* Manila.

[71] ADB. 2019. *Financial Analysis and Evaluation Technical Guidance Note.* Manila.

[72] Footnote 71. Appendix 6: Risk and Sensitivity Analysis.

[73] Footnote 71.

[74] ADB. 2015. Project Financial Reporting and Auditing. *Operations Manual.* OM J7. Manila.

[75] ADB recognizes the use of the International Standards on Auditing (ISA) as issued by the International Auditing and Assurance Standards Board and requires CSOs to engage auditors conforming to ISA. In that connection, ADB also accepts (i) national auditing standards when deemed sufficiently equivalent to ISA, and (ii) the ISA-based International Standards of Supreme Audit Institutions as issued by the International Organization of Supreme Audit Institutions.

Procuring Civil Society Organizations

This section addresses the procurement methods for engaging CSOs to provide nonconsulting and consulting services, publicizing business opportunities to CSOs, framework agreements, TOR and contracting approaches, engagement of CSOs in fragile and conflict-affected situations (FCAS), engaging small CSOs, and advancing funds to CSOs. It also addresses innovative approaches to procurement, such as community participation in procurement, working within the existing ADB procurement guidelines. All procurement of civil works, goods, consulting and nonconsulting services must be in accordance with the ADB Procurement Policy (2017) and the Procurement Regulations for ADB Borrowers (2017), as amended from time to time.[76]

ADB seeks engagement with CSOs within a suite of conditionalities related to effectiveness and efficiency (results-based management, quality control measures, and value for money), high performance (resource allocation mechanisms and payment by results), accountability, transparency, and competition (tendering systems and calls for proposals). Bearing this in mind, when engaging with CSOs, it is important to recognize that CSOs may not have the same experience working with ADB through procurement processes as some commercial consulting firms.

Many CSOs, particularly locally based and small CSOs, struggle to meet donor requirements in terms of proposals, reporting, governance systems, auditing, financial accounts, and staff procedures. Challenges can include the following:

(i) **Proposals and reporting**. CSOs often put grant and proposal writing high on their list of capacity needs—this is high because of the overwhelming reliance of CSOs on donor funding for sustainability. The requirement to produce documents in English and fill in forms with complicated logical frameworks in inaccessible language (including means of verification, objectively verifiable indicators, outcomes and output indicators, impact pathways) puts applying for funding out of the reach of some local CSOs.

(ii) **Online bidding**. Similarly, the requirement to bid online (such as through ADB's CMS) is an onerous requirement for some local CSOs, particularly when internet and electricity connections are patchy.

(iii) **Financial requirements**. Many CSOs struggle to meet donors' financial requirements. Some local CSOs, particularly at the village level, will not have a bank account, let alone audited financial statements. Many CSOs' governance systems are weak, partly due to the lack of paid staff and high levels of volunteerism.[77]

Many CSOs have resource constraints. They may see ADB as a potential source of funding because it is a development bank. It is important to be clear and transparent about the availability of funding and not raise CSOs' expectations of funding.[78]

Engaging CSOs in procurement for ADB-financed projects is a balance. ADB must ensure that its procurement principles of economy, efficiency, fairness, open competition, transparency, quality, and value for money are met. Additionally, CSOs offer particular competencies and added value, and may at times require hand-holding and capacity building for assistance to navigate ADB procurement processes. This hand-holding support, and the form it may take, is discussed later in this section.

---

[76] ADB. 2017. *ADB Procurement Policy: Goods, Works, Nonconsulting and Consulting Services*. Manila; ADB. 2017. *Procurement Regulations for ADB Borrowers: Goods, Works, Nonconsulting and Consulting Services*. Manila.

[77] L.C. Thomas et al. 2019. Participation Tools for the Pacific – Part 1: Engaging Pacific Civil Society Organizations. Development Asia. Manila.

[78] Footnote 77.

A good entry point for CSO engagement in procurement, particularly for larger international CSOs, is the NGOC's business guide: *Working with ADB: A Primer for Identifying Business Opportunities for NGOs*.[79]

Publicizing business opportunities to civil society organizations

DMC officials and project officers should consider how to alert potential CSO bidders (firms or individuals) to the business opportunity. To attract expressions of interest from consulting firms, including CSOs, advertisements may be posted in an appropriate social media channel, or national journal, newspaper, or radio station.

Other methods may also be employed to attract CSOs as bidders, suitable to the context. For example, in some DMCs, advertising by social media may not be suitable, and it may be more appropriate to deliver letters by post or by mainstream media, depending on the resource situation of each DMC. ADB staff and DMC officials should carefully consider the local context and decide what are the appropriate ways to advertise within that DMC so CSOs that may have the capacity to apply, and will learn about the opportunities in good time to do so.

While many firms have experience winning and completing contracts in line with ADB requirements, CSOs have different levels of experience. Thus, ADB staff and DMC staff must ensure that CSOs operating in project areas are well-informed about the possible work opportunities in ADB-financed projects and that bidding CSOs know what resources are available to help them bid for, win, and administer ADB-financed contracts.

Engaging civil society organizations to provide nonconsulting services

CSOs may be engaged under service provider contracts to provide nonconsulting services. Nonconsulting services differ from consulting services (which are services of an intellectual or advisory nature) in that they are services where: (i) the physical aspects of the activity predominate, are bid and contracted on the basis of performance of a measurable physical output, and for which performance standards can be clearly identified and consistently applied; or, (ii) routine services which, while requiring expert inputs, are based on recognized standard offerings that are readily available and which do not require evaluation of tailored methodologies or techniques.[80]

Nonconsulting services provided by CSOs may include providing enumerators or data entry for a water, sanitation, and hygiene (WASH) survey; other surveys; childcare and youth work, long-term care and disability inclusion; services for gender-based violence (GBV) or sexual exploitation, abuse and harassment (SEAH) survivors; workshop or event facilitation; web, social media, and information and communication technology (ICT) surveys; food distribution; asset and cash direct transfer support; contact tracing services for public health; or constructing small-scale infrastructure.

Examples of the types of services where the **physical aspects predominate**, which could be performed by CSOs (includes the use of equipment and specific methodologies to achieve their objectives, such as installation and maintenance services, surveys, and field investigations, information technology implementation services, physical support services):

(i) simple construction works upgrading, small expansions, climate change adaptation (CCA), and maintenance of village and community communal infrastructure, including:
  - community shelter, including urgent repairs to individual dwellings using community participation processes;
  - community and village irrigation;

---

79 ADB. 2018. *Working with ADB: A Primer for Identifying Business Opportunities for NGOs*. Manila
80 ADB. 2017. *Procurement Regulations for ADB Borrowers: Goods, Works, Nonconsulting and Consulting Services*. Manila. para. 1.12; ADB. 2020. *Procurement Staff Instructions*. Manila.

- community water and sanitation work;
- community health facilities;
- access roads, tracks and pathways;
- local schools and training facilities;
- village places of community meetings, gatherings, and worship;
- youth centers, youth workshops, and communal boarding facilities;
- village security posts;
- early warning infrastructure;
- emergency shelters;
- sports centers and facilities; and
- community kitchens and small community livelihood facilities.

(ii) surveys and field investigations;
(iii) ICT equipment;
(iv) medical equipment, supplies, and cleaning material;
(v) delivery of food and water services;
(vi) delivery of maintenance and operational consumables for community facilities (schools, sports centers, and others);
(vii) food distributions;
(viii) simple remote medical facilities;
(ix) provision personal protective equipment, hygiene kits, and isolation wards for care homes and other CSO institutional settings, including CSO-run hospitals and primary health care clinics;
(x) provision of basic need packages (food, nonfood items, care and hygiene kits) for vulnerable groups; and
(xi) provision of supplies for interrupted medical supplies (especially related to noncommunicable disease management and palliative care).

Examples of the types of **routine services requiring expert services**, which could be provided by CSOs (including standard audits, inspections, engineering and quantity surveys, quality assurance certification, vocational training, standardized site surveys, translation or interpretation services, event management, hotel and office rentals, internet services, telecommunication services, website maintenance):
(i) village and community information sharing and gathering;
(ii) capacity building, training, workshops;
(iii) technical and vocational education, and livelihood skills training;
(iv) focus group discussions;
(v) community trauma support;
(vi) disaster preparedness and disaster risk awareness;
(vii) medical services;
(viii) youth work and youth economic empowerment;
(ix) older persons' care and disabled care work;
(x) specific support to vulnerable groups;
(xi) sports facilitation and training;
(xii) health and hygiene awareness raising;
(xiii) support with community legal services, accreditation, or registration;
(xiv) surveys, participatory rapid appraisals, data compilation and analysis;
(xv) website and social media services;
(xvi) information and advocacy campaigns;
(xvii) community participatory planning and design;
(xviii) facilitation of community participation;

(xix) specific awareness raising, consultations with vulnerable groups (women and girls, LGBT+, disabled, youth, aged);

(xx) mentoring of households and community groups;

(xxi) community, school, university, and workplace Sustainable Development Goal (SDG) awareness raising, understanding and action campaigns, such as awareness raising on climate change and green technologies;

(xxii) monitoring and evaluating community activities and behavior change;

(xxiii) event set-up;

(xxiv) distributing direct cash transfers;

(xxv) frontline support for victims or survivors of violence against women and children (e.g., counselling, emergency housing, legal advice);

(xxvi) translation support;

(xxvii) auditing of food distribution and direct cash transfer programs;

(xxviii) awareness materials for hard-to-reach groups;

(xxix) support technology, data collection and analysis for field level monitoring of impact of coronavirus disease (COVID-19) on vulnerable groups;

(xxx) translation and training materials for community groups and service providers (care providers, family caregivers);

(xxxi) guidelines and protocols on COVID-19 and high-risk groups (older persons, underlying health conditions, people in institutions); and

(xxxii) technology inputs for monitoring, provision of social services remotely, and hotlines.

Engaging civil society organizations as consulting firms

CSOs may be engaged in all capacities that firms can be engaged. ADB defines "consulting firm" as any entity with the capacity to provide consulting services; this includes CSOs, when such entities provide consulting services.[81] Therefore, CSOs can be engaged to provide consulting services.

When recruiting a CSO as a TA or project consultant, project officers must follow all ADB requirements for procuring consulting firms. Under these requirements, when engaging CSOs for assignments where their unique experience and qualifications provide better value to the project, modified approaches may be considered, such as the following:

(i) **Simplified quality- and cost-based selection for national civil society organizations**. When hiring national CSOs as consulting firms, particularly for cases when specialist community knowledge, experience in participatory approaches, or local expertise is sought, a modified (simplified) quality- and cost-based selection recruitment method is used. The evaluation criteria will reflect (a) history of work with local communities and evidence of satisfactory performance, (b) familiarity with participatory development approaches, (c) committed leadership and adequate management, and (d) capacity to co-opt beneficiary participation.[82]

(ii) **Direct contracting for civil society organization recruitment in special circumstances**. Direct contracting, also known as single-source selection, may be used as a recruitment method for CSOs under special circumstances. Direct contracting does not provide the benefits of competition and lacks transparency. However, it may be used only if this method provides a clear advantage over other

---

[81] ADB. 2020. Definitions, Principles and Responsibilities. *Project Administration Instructions*. PAI 2.01. Manila; and ADB. 2020. *Procurement Staff Instructions*. Manila.

[82] Note that this provision is only applicable for projects approved before 1 July 2017 as the 2017 Procurement Policy applies to all projects with concept notes approved on or after 1 July 2017 and does not contain this provision.

competitive recruitment methods. Situations where direct contracting may provide this advantage are set out in the Procurement Regulations.[83]

ADB offers six selection methods for engaging firms, which also apply to CSOs. Each selection method offers opportunities and challenges for engaging CSOs. Refer to the ADB Procurement Regulations (2017)[84] for further information.

(i) **Quality- and cost-based selection**. This method is used when equal weight is given to the quality of a technical proposal and the proposed contract cost as provided in the financial proposal. The quality- and cost-based selection (QCBS) is appropriate when (a) the scope of the work can be precisely defined, (b) the TOR are clearly defined, and (c) the consultants can estimate with reasonable accuracy the personnel time and other inputs needed. Consider also that because QCBS can be complex and resource intensive, it may discourage CSOs from bidding. Consider using QCBS for large contracts where large international CSOs with sufficient resources for proposal preparation are likely to bid.

(ii) **Quality-based selection**. This method is used when only the quality of a technical proposal is evaluated. The quality-based selection (QBS) is appropriate when (a) assignments are complex or highly specialized, making it difficult to define TORs and the required inputs from consultants, (b) the downstream impact of the assignment is so large that the quality of the services is of overriding importance for the outcome of the project, and (c) assignments can be carried out in very different ways such that financial proposals may be difficult to compare. QBS is typically appropriate for CSOs who will bring specific technical inputs, such as scientific expertise, for example, in areas such as food safety, knowledge of regional freight forwarding systems, or delivery of vaccination awareness raising programs or community behavior change programs.

(iii) **Consultant qualification selection**. The consultant qualification selection (CQS) method can be used for small assignments ($200,000 or less) where highly specialized expertise is required and few consultants are qualified. Under CQS, only the most qualified shortlisted firm is invited to submit a full proposal. The process for selection is simpler than other methods. Use CQS, for example, when small-scale specific inputs are required from few consultants, for example, for a technical review of technical and vocational education curricula in a specific subject area (e.g., motor vehicle repair).

(iv) **Direct contracting**. This method is often the most appropriate for engaging CSOs when their niche expertise is critical. One criterion for using direct contracting is for small assignments. Direct contracting is also justified when only one firm is qualified or has experience of high worth for the assignment. ADB engages CSOs through direct contracting because of their specific qualifications for a task. Typical situations where direct contracting is used to recruit CSOs is where the CSO is the only organization with direct links to the target communities; or is the only organization qualified to undertake the task, for example, a nurses association providing professional development to its members; or has undertaken the first phase of a two-phase program and is the only organization qualified to undertake the second phase.

(v) **Fixed-budget selection**. The fixed-budget selection (FBS) is a competitive selection method, where the budget is fixed, and the bid is not evaluated on price. FBS allows bidders to offer the most resources for the budget available. It may be a suitable selection method for CSOs as they may be able to propose resources beyond those called for in the TOR. Situations where FBS may be used include where the TOR is precisely defined, the personnel and other inputs are able to be accurately assessed, and the budget for the services is enough for completion of the task or service. This method may be appropriate for standardized and discrete services suitable for CSOs, such as providing a rapid

---

83 ADB. 2017. *Procurement Regulations for ADB Borrowers: Goods, Works, Nonconsulting and Consulting Services*. Manila.
84 Footnote 83.

assessment report of the state of waste management services in a particular location, or conducting willingness-to-pay studies.

(vi) **Least-cost selection**. This is the appropriate method for selecting consultants for small assignments of a standard or routine nature and where there are well-established practices and standards (e.g., audit or inspection services). This method is suited for small assignments which CSOs may be able to deliver, such as providing local enumerators for a sanitation and hygiene awareness study of a local community, or providing facilitation services for a series of community or stakeholder meetings.

Helping civil society organizations help ADB. To engage CSOs as consultants, it may be necessary to incorporate capacity-building support for CSOs to acclimatize them to ADB procurement processes. Budget for this should be incorporated into project preparation or project implementation costs. If CSO engagement is to occur in ADB-financed operations, the potential CSO consultants or service providers must become accustomed to ADB processes. It is important to note that providing this capacity support and engagement with ADB and the DMC government may strengthen the CSO's own processes and governance. Such capacity-building support could include

(i) scoping CSO capacity to deliver project components as part of transaction TA and designing the transaction TA accordingly;

(ii) offering training to potential CSO bidders on ADB's procurement processes—this should be budgeted as part of transaction TA;

(iii) incorporating CSO capacity-building into loan and grant agreements at the start of project implementation, prior to the recruitment of consultants;

(iv) adopting realistic schedules to ensure that a generous timeframe is allocated for CSO recruitment;

(v) support local CSOs with administration of ADB-financed operations, by budgeting for employment of administration expert(s) experienced in ADB-financed operations;

(vi) offering capacity-building support and close guidance to local CSOs by the resident mission (i.e., a CSO anchor in the resident mission assisting a local CSO with CMS registration);

(vii) providing online or face-to-face training on procurement and CMS processes (particularly considering any potential technology or language barriers); and

(viii) contracting larger CSOs to work with and build the capacity of smaller CSOs.

It is important to ensure that CSOs also understand ADB's consultant performance evaluation review process, which is completed at the end of consulting assignments when ADB recruits consulting firms for TA and staff consulting, or when ADB recruits individual consultants for TA, staff, training, and resource person assignments. PAI 2.07 details the instructions and the CSO should be directed to familiarize itself with this process.[85]

Box 11, introduced earlier, outlines an example of this capacity support provided to support CSO engagement in transaction TA.

The following case study illustrates the value of ensuring that CSOs understand the complexities of ADB procurement processes.

---

[85] ADB. 2020. Consultant Performance Evaluation. *Project Administration Instructions*. PAI 2.07. Manila.

BOX 16

The Coral Triangle Initiative is a $15 million regional TA which used single-source selection to procure the services of three CSOs across five countries (Fiji, Papua New Guinea, Solomon Islands, Timor-Leste, Vanuatu). The three CSOs were implementing various subprojects in the TA addressing issues, including coastal management planning, installing, and training fishers on the use of fish aggregating devices; livelihood and CCA initiatives; capacity building; and establishing protected areas and seascape planning. Single-source selection was chosen as the preferred mode of engagement for three reasons:

    (i)   the CSOs demonstrated exceptional qualities in their respective areas of expertise in integrated coastal management and ecosystem-based management,

    (ii)   the activities were a natural continuation of work previously done by the CSOs, and

    (iii) the CSOs had good working relationships with government, and government was confident in the CSO's ability to deliver results.

The time taken to engage the CSOs via single source selection was considerable (20 months) and required approval for the use of single source selection, various approvals to engage each of the three CSOs followed by requests for proposals, evaluations, contract negotiations and notices to proceed. The time-taken to go through this process led to the delay of some of the subprojects that the CSOs were to deliver. One of the key reasons for delay was that the CSOs were not fully aware of the terms of the standard form of ADB contracts, and contract negotiation took a considerable amount of time. ADB staff report that it would be helpful to a) offer training to CSOs on ADB contracting procedures, and financial management (expense monitoring, disbursement forecasting) and procurement processes which were also challenging during implementation; and b) review ADB's own systems and processes for how these could enable more efficient project implementation and partnerships with CSOs, in recognition of their differences to consulting firms.

Overall, working with the CSOs provided the following benefits to the TA:

    (i)   The CSOs had established relationships and networks and worked closely with the respective communities.

    (ii)   They had deep country knowledge and technical expertise (where they had the staff capacity).

    (iii) They were motivated and demonstrated high levels of integrity (such as refusing additional work because the timeframes were too tight or doing so would have undermined the methodology).

ADB = Asian Development Bank, CCA = climate change adaptation, CSO = civil society organization, TA = technical assistance.
Source: D. Robertson. 2017. *Engaging with NGOs on Coral Triangle of the Pacific: Our project team's experience of processes, positives, pits and tips.* Presentation given during the ADB–Government–CSO workshop. Samoa. 11 September.

Framework agreements

In line with ADB procurement procedures, CSOs can be recruited under a framework agreement. A framework agreement is awarded pursuant to one of the methods set out in ADB's procurement regulations between one or more contracting authorities and one or more contractors, suppliers, or service providers. The purpose of the agreement is to establish the terms governing contracts to be awarded during a given period, particularly regarding price and, where appropriate, the quantity envisaged. The framework agreement also sets out terms and conditions under which specific procurements or service provisions (known as "call-offs") can be made throughout the term of the agreement.[86] Framework agreements may be suitable for services or goods that CSOs provide across a region or sector or event, such as a disaster response.

Executing agencies can select CSOs or firms through framework agreements for multiple, planned consultancy assignments under the agreement for consulting services described in ADB's *Procurement Regulations for ADB Borrowers: Goods, Works, Nonconsulting and Consulting Services* (2017).[87]

This is for engagements that
    (i)   belong to a category of technically or thematically similar assignments,
    (ii)   require similar expertise,
    (iii)   can be repeated,
    (iv)   can be described with broad TOR,
    (v)   are for a defined time period,
    (vi)   will be implemented in one or more locations ranging from a single country to multiple regions, and
    (vii) in cases where the exact scope and location are not known at the time of awarding the contract.[88]

When using framework agreements or procurement agreements, a government executing agency selects a pool of consultants ready to be engaged when services are needed. The agreement is, therefore, not a contract as there is no obligation for the executing agency to provide consulting work and no obligation from the consultants to provide their services. The purpose is to engage consultants through specific contracts when there is a need. The administration of an agreement is subject to ADB procurement rules.

For example, a government executing agency could develop an agreement with CSOs who are familiar with the geographical area listed in the country programming documents and who have mobilized participation among poor and disadvantaged individuals in community development in these areas in the past, or who have technical expertise in poverty reduction and community development strategies needed in multiple programs or projects. When these kinds of consultancy services are needed, the government executing agency can easily contract these CSOs through an agreement. The main advantage is search and selection takes less time. It is important for the government executing agency to work with ADB to make sure that the development and administration of agreements follow ADB procurement rules.

Framework agreements can be closed or open, and exclusive or nonexclusive, as outlined in Table 9.

---

[86]   Footnote 83.
[87]   Footnote 83. Integrity due diligence will be undertaken and the Office of Anticorruption and Integrity (OAI) should be consulted on the scope of integrity due diligence, as appropriate.
[88]   ADB. 2018. *Framework Agreements for Consulting Services: Guidance Note on Procurement*. Manila.

Table 9: Comparison of Framework Agreements

Closed agreements Only the originally selected consultants are considered for the time frame of the agreement. The executing agency closes the framework agreement to new consultants, which gives the selected consultants a good chance of getting a contract.	**Open agreements** New consultants can be added during the time frame of the agreement. The disadvantage of this agreement is the executing agency's increased administrative workload of considering new applicants.
Exclusive agreements The executing agency intends to use only the agreement consultants for contracts of the type described in the agreement.	**Nonexclusive agreements** The executing agency reserves the right to award contracts of the type described under the agreement outside of the framework agreement, at their sole discretion

Source: ADB. 2018. Framework Agreements for Consulting Services: Guidance Note on Procurement. Manila. p.9.

An example framework agreement for procuring CSOs is in Appendix 3.

Output-based contracts and terms of reference

ADB uses two types of TOR: input-based (time) and output-based (performance). In an input-based TOR, the project officer defines the inputs, which is typically a list of the consultants, the expertise they need to have, and the length of time each is needed.

In an output-based TOR, the project officer defines only the output required, and allows the bidding entities to propose the inputs and approach they will use to deliver the output.

Output-based or lump sum remuneration schemes are preferable to input-based schemes for ADB.[89] These may also be more familiar and preferable to CSOs, because they require less documentation for eligible expenses than input-based contracts. The output-based remuneration should be clearly stated in the TOR. In addition, preparing output-based TOR may also allow bidding CSOs to build a team based on the expertise they have available and incorporate the approaches they believe are best suited to address the assignment.

An output-based TOR may be the better choice when engaging a CSO because
- (i)   the CSO will apply its local knowledge to how the output can be best delivered, knowledge which the project officer may not have and
- (ii) the CSO can propose staff who have cross-cutting skill sets appropriate for the task and who are readily available.

The project officer needs to mitigate certain risks when using an output-based TOR, including the following:
- (i)   Not having specific enough deliverables that are clearly measurable. A TOR without clear deliverables should be prepared as an input-based TOR.
- (ii) Not having enough of the key skills. The project officer should specify a few key experts the proposing entity should include. Examples include the team leader, technical expert(s), and an administrative and finance officer.

---

[89]   ADB. 2020. *Technical Assistance Disbursement Handbook.* Manila.

An output-based TOR is appropriate when the bidding entity should propose how to deliver the project and what inputs are needed to deliver it. This style of TOR is useful for contracting CSOs, as CSOs are accustomed to designing their approaches and activities.

Since most TOR are input-based, use these tips to advertise an output-based TOR:

(i) In the CMS:
- Indicate if the key experts will be international or national.
- Insert a dummy date into the CMS for the key experts, such as 0.25 months.

(ii) In the TOR:
- State that the indicated length for the key experts is a dummy date and that the bidding entity should propose how many person-months are actually needed.
- Indicate that in addition to the required key experts, the proposing organizations should list all the other non-key experts they will provide to complete the project.

Note that an output TOR is possible even if the TA paper or RRP include specific positions. It may be better to ask for a full or simplified technical proposal instead of a biodata proposal to ensure bidding entities provide sufficient details of exactly how they propose to carry out the project. Remember: every procurement package is different, and the procurement risks vary from project to project. Always consult with the procurement team in the Procurement, Portfolio, and Financial Management Department (PPFD) to make sure the style of the TOR is appropriate to the situation.

Contracting selected civil society organizations

ADB uses five types of contracts:

(i) indefinite delivery contract,
(ii) lump sum contract,
(iii) performance-based or output-based contract,
(iv) retainer or contingency fee contract, and
(v) time-based contract.

When looking to engage CSOs, consider offering a performance- or output-based contract with payments made upon ADB's acceptance of deliverables. Lump sum payments (see Box 17) to a consultant are triggered by the achievement of selected milestones signifying that certain project deliverables have been completed (e.g., an output or outcome defined in the project design or monitoring agreement). This type of contract allows CSOs to adjust their project inputs to changing conditions to better deliver their outputs. Therefore, milestones need to be clearly specified and sufficient in number for effective monitoring and verification.

The standard forms of payment for consultants are time-based and lump sum contracts. Lump sum contracts are easier to administer.

Time-based contracts

Under time-based contracts, fees are paid, and expenses reimbursed based on expenditures or time spent during the implementation. Billings are usually monthly. For organizational efficiency, ADB uses mobilization payment, milestone payments, and final statement of eligible costs payment in time-based contracts with consulting entities (including CSOs). These payments are calculated as percentage of experts' time. At the end of the contract implementation, the payments made are reconciled against actual time spent (based on the time sheets submitted monthly) in a process called Final Statement of Eligible Costs. Out-of-pocket expenses are billed monthly. ADB borrowers use time-based contracts with monthly billings based on actual time spent (certified by the time sheets) and out-of-pocket expenses incurred during the period. For consulting services, consider the use of fixed out-of-pocket expenses, for administrative efficiency and to simplify the disbursement process.

Time-based contracts are recommended when the scope of the services may need to be adjusted during implementation or when the duration and quantity of services depend on variables that are beyond the control of the consultant. This type of contract requires the executing agency or ADB to closely supervise the consultant and to be involved in the daily execution of the assignment.

Lump sum contracts

Under lump sum contracts, payments are made to the CSO as a percentage of the total contract at agreed times or on the completion of clearly defined stages of work. This may entail a percentage on completion of inception activities (such as mobilization of key staff to complete the assignment and submission of an inception report), a further payment on successful completion of a mid-project milestone or series of milestones defined in the scope of assignment. Lump sum contracts are useful when the output is clearly defined and there is little room for dispute as to whether the work has been satisfactorily completed or not. Lump sum contracts are easier to supervise than time-based contracts, since the lump sum contracts do not need so much oversight and accounting. They may be considered appropriate for any type of selection system, but are especially useful for QCBS, FBS, LCS, and CQS.

The decision about which type of contract to use should be mutually agreed between the executing agency or ADB and the CSO. The decision will often depend on how well the issues surrounding the proposal have been resolved and how accurately the inputs and expenditures in the proposal have been clarified. If there are "gray areas" about the inputs, but the outputs are well defined, it may be better to use a lump sum contract. On the other hand, if the inputs (or at least unit rates) are clearly agreed upon, but the outputs are uncertain, then a time-based contract may be better. In either case, the decision taken at this point should be seen as temporary. During the final negotiations, those involved might agree to switch to a different contract type.

continued on next page

Box 17 continued

Besides time-based and lump sum contracts, three other types of contracts are possible: retainer and/or contingency fee contracts, indefinite delivery contracts, and performance-based contracts. These are not used as often as time-based and lump sum contracts, and there are no formal standard contract documents for them. For TA-funded assignments, ADB uses the same contract document for both time-based and lump sum contracts.

Bear in mind that use of a nonconsulting modality (service provision contracts) may be more suitable for the types of engagements with CSOs.

ADB = Asian Development Bank, CQS = consultant qualification selection, CSO = civil society organization, FBS = fixed-budget selection, LCS = least-cost selection, QCBS = quality- and cost-based selection.
Source: ADB. 2008. *Consulting Services Operations Manual*. Manila. pp. 95–96.

The following points will make the execution of the agreed-upon activities and deliverables easier when engaging CSOs:

(i)   Make sure the contract provides a clear list of expected outputs, details about coordination with the ADB project team leader and staff and any government PMU, and payment release arrangements. Even minor misunderstandings can delay payments and cause frustration on all sides.

(ii)   When finalizing the contract, consider national and local laws, plus financial and procurement rules and procedures that a CSO consultant must comply with to be able to execute its contract on ADB-financed projects.

(iii)   Before implementation, make sure the CSO understands the procurement and disbursement policies and guidelines of ADB, including the *Technical Assistance Disbursement Handbook* (2010, as amended from time to time). In the case of loan and grants, make sure the CSO is clear on the procurement and disbursement policies of the DMC government. Offer to answer questions and provide support in managing the contract beyond normal requirements. As many CSOs have never worked with ADB, they may need more support than a private firm that has been an ADB partner on previous projects. The financial requirements of an ADB contract are likely to differ from a CSO's contracts with other donors more than the contracts that a private sector consultancy firm typically executes.

(iv)   Ensure the CSO understands what are eligible and ineligible expenditures. Indirect costs, like cost recoveries, markups, and management fees, do not meet the definition of "direct and identifiable" to the TA account and, therefore, do not meet requirement of "eligible expenditures." Refer to OM H3 Cost Sharing and Eligibility of Expenditures for ADB Financing which lays out criteria for eligible expenditures for ADB's own resources and for funds administered by ADB.[90]

(v)   Carefully assess the competency needs of the CSO and help them develop any required competencies. An ADB project officer or DMC official can support a CSO more effectively by being fully aware of a CSO's financial and technical capacities.

(vi)   Make sure there is a timely flow of funds with a CSO. It helps to include in the inception report a proposed cost estimate of each planned activity for a one-time approval by the Technical Assistance Supervising Unit or User Unit. For approval to use the advance, the CSO must have adequate administrative and accounting capacity to establish enough internal controls, accounting and auditing procedures. If the capacity of the CSO is determined to be inadequate, the advance fund procedure should not be used. Instead, another disbursement method, such as direct payment, may need to

---

[90]   ADB. 2017. Cost Sharing and Eligibility of Expenditures for ADB Financing. *Operations Manual*. OM H3. Manila.

be considered. A request for advance must be supported by a detailed estimate of the expenditure requirements for specific activities or procurement to be financed through the TA account. (Refer to the *Technical Assistance Disbursement Handbook,* sections 5.11 and 5.12 (ii) Advance Procedure.) Cash advances for each activity should be released no less than 2 weeks before the scheduled implementation. Within 30 days after the completion of the activities for which the advance was provided, supporting documentation should be submitted to substantiate the advance. Subsequent advances will be provided only once previous advances are fully or substantially liquidated. (Refer to the *Technical Assistance Disbursement Handbook,* section 5.13 Liquidation.)

Procurement in fragile and conflict-affected situations

With the approval of the DMC government, ADB may work with CSOs as implementing entities if the government does not have the qualified human resources to fill these roles. CSO assignments as implementing entities are subject to appropriate and satisfactory financial management assessment and integrity due diligence, with results acceptable to PPFD (for financial management assessment) and the Office of Anticorruption and Integrity (OAI) (for integrity due diligence).

Where institutional capacity is weak, ADB may consider a request of the borrower to contract CSOs to undertake all or part of project implementation, including the procurement function. CSOs may also be engaged in FCAS as consultants to assist the borrower where capacity is weak. This may also be as a management consultant to the borrower to assist with the selection, contract negotiations, and contract management of suppliers, contractors, and consultants in situations where the possibility of corruption is high.[91]

For details on procurement in FCAS, refer to ADB's 2018 *Fragile, Conflict-Affected and Emergency Situations Guidance Note on Procurement.*

Engaging small civil society organizations

While locally based CSOs often understand their communities' needs and can provide an excellent link between ADB, DMC governments, and local people, ADB and member governments can face challenges in engaging these locally based or small CSOs in ADB-financed operations. These challenges include

(i)   low capacity to engage with ADB through the CMS,

(ii)   limited access to the internet and/or English language skills, and

(iii)   minimal capacity to respond to ADB and DMC's calls for expressions of interest or request for tender.

This section below provides examples of these situations and some innovative approaches to address these challenges.

Corporations and companies must be incorporated or legally established to be recruited by ADB as consultants. CSOs that are not incorporated must provide details that they are duly established with the legal capacity to enter into binding and enforceable contracts with ADB.[92] In situations where small CSOs, such as community-based organizations, do not meet these requirements, project officers can consider (i) engaging a larger (legally registered) CSO that may then provide support to the smaller CSOs, as well as manage funds disbursement to the smaller CSOs; or (ii) engaging an umbrella or peak organization, of which the small CSO is a member.

---

[91]   ADB. 2018. *Fragile, Conflict-Affected and Emergency Situations Guidance Note on Procurement.* Manila.

[92]   ADB. 2020. Specific Requirements for Recruiting Consultants by ADB. *Project Administration Instructions.* PAI 2.04. Manila.

In addition, these organizations, particularly grassroots CSOs, can be engaged using service provider contracts for nonconsulting services, which are not processed through the consultant management system and not signed by PPFD.

Advancing funds to civil society organizations

CSOs may have few unallocated funds. All resources are linked to specific projects and activities. Therefore, ADB staff and PMUs must design a payment schedule to ensure that enough funds are released in the initial payment (tranche) for the CSO to pay for staff and start activities. CSOs typically do not have their own funds for these expenses the way private firms that earn profit do.

A CSO may not be accustomed to working as a contractor as most receive their funds through grants. A CSO usually designs a project, submits a proposal to a funding agency, and then implements the project according to the plan in the proposal. Funding agencies usually allow CSOs some flexibility in the use of funds, some changes to the approach and to objectives and outputs as they would if dealing with a partner. ADB staff and PMUs must clearly communicate to CSOs the difference between this way of working and implementing an ADB-financed contract. When delivering a contract, the CSO is expected to complete the contract as designed by ADB or the implementing agency and not "as they see fit."

When it comes to funds, a CSO may be accustomed to a different level of accountability than ADB requires. Some donor agencies, such as the United Kingdom's Foreign, Commonwealth & Development Office, GIZ, and SIDA allow for some spending flexibility if the objectives are being achieved. ADB requirements are more complex and ADB staff and PMUs must make sure that CSOs are prepared for this. Staff and PMUs may, for example, make payments dependent on deliverables.

In FCAS, securing a bank guarantee to guarantee the advanced funds may prove challenging. In such cases, ADB and DMC staff need to conduct a risk assessment, provide options and risk mitigation measures. The CSO's track record of implementing similar works with other donors, development partners, and government, including local government, may also be considered. For example, contracts with CSOs with track records of good performance may be offered the payment of an appropriate amount of advance without being required to provide a bank guarantee.[93]

Innovative approaches to procurement of civil society organizations

Working within the established ADB procurement policy and guidelines, ADB and DMC government officials can use innovative approaches to working with CSOs. Examples include the following:
  (i)   Community Participation in Procurement.
  (ii)   Contracting an international CSO or large national CSO through consulting services to implement a competitive community awards program with small or locally based CSOs.
  (iii) Using innovative procurement processes for procuring small CSOs.

93   Footnote 91.

Community participation in procurement

To achieve a project's social objectives or sustainability, CSOs are eligible to participate in the community participation in procurement method.[94] CSOs engaged using this method may deliver services or small-scale civil works. PAI 3.07 details the procurement procedures.[95]

Community participation in procurement as described in ADB's 2017 *Procurement Regulations for ADB Borrowers*:

> *2.36 Where, in the interest of project sustainability or to achieve certain specific social objectives of the project, it is desirable under selected project components to call for the participation of local communities and/or nongovernment organizations in the delivery of services, the procurement procedures, specifications, and contract packaging shall be suitably adapted to reflect these considerations, provided these are efficient and result in value for money.[96]*

Community participation in procurement has been used in ADB for engaging local communities in community construction works for subprojects in ADB-financed projects[97] (such as drains, small schools, road maintenance, and others), and may or may not engage CSOs. However, this mechanism may also be used to engage CSOs or the community to deliver services on an ADB-financed project and to increase the utilization of local knowledge on ADB-financed operations.

Two case studies on this approach are presented below:

BOX 18

The **Afghanistan Community-Based Irrigation Rehabilitation and Development Project**[a] used the community participation in procurement method to assist local farmers, through their community development councils (CDCs) and with the support of the Department of Rural Rehabilitation and Development (DRRD), plan and develop irrigation facilities. The project also tapped NGOs to assist the Ministry of Rural Rehabilitation and Development in strengthening the capacity of provincial staff of the DRRD. NGOs trained them in orienting, mobilizing, and organizing rural communities. This activity helped the local government officers guide and support the CDCs during project implementation. One hundred fifty-one civil works contracts through community participation have been awarded with total 151 subprojects completed. The project reaped gains beyond what it had expected or planned. It generated jobs for the people, creating about 270,000 person-days in short-term employment, approximately equivalent to roughly $2.5 million in wages. In the process, more than 180,000 households or over 1.4 million CDC members benefited from the rehabilitation activities and the jobs generated by the project.

continued on next page

---

[94] Footnote 83.
[95] ADB. 2018. Procurement Methods in Special Circumstances and Other Procurement Arrangements. *Project Administration Instructions.* PAI 3.07. Manila.
[96] Footnote 83. p. 20.
[97] ADB. 2018. "How Can We Use Community Contracting More Widely" Hans Woldring on Insight Thursday. 6 Feb 2018.

Box 18 continued

The PNG Rural Primary Health Services Delivery Project strengthened rural health systems in selected areas of PNG by expanding the coverage and improving the quality of primary health care in partnership with the state and other service providers, including CSOs. The project's Output 5 is "Health promotion in local communities." Under this output, the project team designed and implemented a small competitive community awards program for health promotion, using the community participation in procurement method. The small competitive community awards program was designed and delivered in 2013–2018. The project financed small awards to CBOs and local CSOs for identified health promotion priorities. The focus was maternal and child health, HIV, sanitation, gender, and prevention of gender-based violence. The grantees delivered locally identified interventions, including village health volunteer trainings, sexual and reproductive health workshops, a workshop on men's health and well-being, and health promotion activities through drama and song. Seven hundred community members participated in small, localized activities.[b]

To find out more about CSO engagement in the PNG Rural Primary Health Services Delivery Project, view this video: https://www.adb.org/news/videos/adb-and-csos-bring-rural-health-services-papua-new-guinea.

CBO = community-based organization, CSO = civil society organization, NGO = nongovernment organization, PNG = Papua New Guinea.
[a] ADB placed on hold its assistance in Afghanistan effective 15 August 2021.
[b] ADB. Papua New Guinea: Rural Primary Health Services Delivery Project.
Source: Asian Development Bank.

Tips and guidance. Implementing small projects with community participation and coordinated by an implementing agency:

(i) Ensure the procurement method is clearly articulated in the PAM, including the community participation in procurement method and the approach to identifying, calling for proposals, and engaging with the local CSOs.

(ii) Describe in the PAM the TOR method and approach for cost estimates, fund flows, contracting, and others.

(iii) Ensure the mechanism under community participation in procurement is included in the loan agreement.

(iv) Be prepared to advance funds to the CSOs as they will likely require a positive cash flow. The cash flow to a CSO under a TA-financed project and a loan or grant may differ, as TA disbursement is made by ADB, whereas implementing agencies manage disbursements for loans and grants.

(v) Ensure that the implementing agency has adequate "buy-in" to administer the community participation in procurement program.

(vi) Provide support to the implementing agency in the administrative processes and capacity-building on working with CSOs under community participation in procurement.

(vii) Provide capacity-building or mentoring support to the local CSOs on proposal writing, budgeting, reporting, and acquittals. Build this capacity-building support in as a necessary cost of administering small projects with community participation and include this provision in the loan agreement with the borrower.

(viii) Engender a climate of interest and excitement about involvement in the program. Record and celebrate the strengths and achievements of successfully implemented projects. Engage in information and communication dissemination about the program (e.g., video documentaries) to celebrate the achievements and successes of the local CSOs engaged, to create a climate of interest for future programs. Ask previous successful participating CSOs to give case study demonstrations on their work. Consider offering awards for the outstanding activities implemented. Consider ways to support a community of practice for locally focused activities conducted by small CSOs or CBOs.

Contracting an international CSO or large national CSO through consulting services to implement a competitive community awards program with small, locally based CSOs

The second contracting method is to design a community-based competitive awards program and seek an international or large national CSO to deliver this. The international or large national CSO may be procured competitively through consulting services (e.g., QCBS or QBS), but may also be procured through direct contracting (single-source selection). The TOR for the CSO should provide detailed scope of work, outputs or activities, and implementation arrangements for the CSO to implement a small grants program with small and locally based CSOs.

BOX 19

The TA **Mainstreaming Climate Resilience into Development Planning – Cambodia,**[a] approved in 2012, sought to build capacity in integrating climate resilience at national, subnational and community levels. Output 3 was *"Civil society support mechanism established, and capacity of NGOs and CSOs to mainstream CCA and DRR into their operations strengthened."* A competitive community awards program was established under this output. The objectives of the civil society support mechanism, implemented over April 2015 to August 2018, was to implement community-based CCA and DRR activities and strengthen capacity of CSOs to mainstream CCA and DRR into their operations. A further objective was to deliver tangible knowledge outputs. The focus was on "learning by doing" to enhance local capacity. Grantees introduced mangrove rehabilitation, climate-smart agricultural techniques, rehabilitation of climate-resilient community ponds, climate-proofing of houses, ecotourism-related assets, and low-maintenance water purification devices in schools. The capacity of CSOs was measured and organizational capacity gains were demonstrated across seven domains.

The *large CSO to small CSOs model* was effective, achieving all project outputs. The coordinating CSO, Plan International, understood how to communicate and engage with locally based CSOs. Locally based organizations proved very cost-effective with different CSOs bringing different strengths and approaches to the project. There was an iterative process of refinement of proposals between Plan International and the local CSOs. ADB undertook additional reviews and was able to ensure an appropriate balance of geography and intervention type. Toward the end of the project, funds were redistributed from underspending to strongly performing CSOs. Young people were brought into the project by the global youth organization, AIESEC, to help develop knowledge products, although financial issues meant international youth could not be paired with Cambodian youth. A total of 56,612 beneficiaries were involved in project activities, of which 53% were women. ADB's Youth for Asia supported the engagement of young people under this TA.

ADB = Asian Development Bank, CCA = climate change adaptation, CSO = civil society organization, DRR = disaster risk reduction, NGO = nongovernment organization, TA = technical assistance.
[a] ADB. Cambodia: Mainstreaming Climate Resilience into Development Planning.
Source: Asian Development Bank.

Tips and guidance:

(i) Assess the capacity of local and international CSOs to coordinate and deliver a small competitive awards program during project design.

(ii) Identify the procurement method for the coordinating CSO and incorporate this into the PAM. QCBS provides ADB and borrowers with an appropriate balance between quality and cost, and is the method used in the Cambodia case study. Other suitable procurement methods are QBS (prioritizing quality ahead of cost) and direct contracting (when only one CSO is qualified or has exceptional worth for the assignment).

(iii) Detail in the PAM the mechanism and process, including participation of local communities and/or CSOs.

(iv) Hold an information session with potential coordinating CSOs to ensure they are made aware of standard ADB contract terms and ADB bidding, contracting, and financial processes.

(v) If required, provide intensive mentoring support to the successful coordinating CSO on ADB processes. Recognize that the coordinating CSO may not be as experienced in working with ADB as commercial firms.

(vi) Use a performance-based TOR and an output-based contract, with milestones and deliverables evenly spread throughout the contract term.

(vii) Be prepared to advance funds to the CSO as they will likely require a positive cash flow; design this into the process.

The following text[98] may be adapted for use in the PAM for this form of competitive community awards program:

1 *The aim is to support mainstreaming adaptation in the operation of civil society organizations (CSOs). The NGO will be competitively selected following the quality- and cost-based selection method, using the quality–cost ratio of 90:10 and full technical proposal procedures. A detailed scope of work and terms of reference will be developed to advertise and solicit interest. Criteria for selection include:*

   (i) *Official registration with the Government of [DMC] and a collaborative CSO body such as the [insert name of a relevant umbrella organization];*

   (ii) *Adaptation experience at the commune, district, province, and country levels;*

   (iii) *Ability to work constructively with line agencies in support of government policies;*

   (iv) *Experience in running a small competitive community awards scheme coordinating and monitoring community-based projects, and in providing capacity building to local CSOs on mainstreaming adaptation and disaster risk reduction in their operations;*

   (v) *Evidence of sufficient administrative, accounting, and financial management capacity to implement the grant scheme and oversee implementation;*

   (vi) *Commitment to working with vulnerable communities in an inclusive manner; and*

   (vii) *Ability to recruit skilled staff as necessary.*

2 *The NGO will have at least 4 staff members, each with a minimum 5 years of experience in managing and guiding adaptation projects in [DMC] and other countries in the region, and each possessing a bachelor's degree or higher in environmental management, climate change, or related area. The NGO will work under the guidance of the [DMC agency] coordination team and will facilitate issuing calls for proposals to CSOs in [DMC] for adaptation activities that can be funded up to $XX,000 per proposal. Specific criteria and methods of selection will be developed by the entity and approved by ADB and the [DMC agency] coordination team prior to issuing the call for proposals. The activities will focus on: research and knowledge generation on the impacts of climate change in [DMC], and adaptation strategies by community-based*

---

[98] ADB. 2012. *Technical Assistance to Cambodia for Mainstreaming Climate Resilience into Development Planning.* Manila.

organizations; and applying lessons learned from community-based adaptation initiatives to develop additional projects. The NGO will:

(i) *Propose eligibility criteria for grant funding in close cooperation with the [DMC agency] coordination team and the technical backstopping unit;*

(ii) *Provide advice on the design and implementation of the selected CSO initiatives;*

(iii) *Perform independent assessments of the funded initiatives; and*

(iv) *Share lessons learned and document the initiatives as case studies.*

Innovation in procurement of small CSOs

Small CSOs may find it difficult to navigate ADB's procurement processes. One option to address this is to adopt an innovative approach to attract the participation in procurement of smaller CSOs. The approach described in this section is that of a two-stage process: an open call for proposals, with proposals then evaluated and ranked; and then selection of the successful CSOs through direct contracting. Detailed and specific support was provided to the CSOs at both stages of the process.

The TA Mitigating the Impact of COVID-19 through Community-Led Interventions[99] directly supports CSOs to scale-up or expand their ongoing health-focused interventions to alleviate the negative consequences of the pandemic on these poor and vulnerable groups and their communities. With the view to enticing a wide pool of CSOs, both large and small, to participate in the TA, a different approach to the procurement process was adopted. The starting point was a Call for Project Concepts that opened up the field to smaller, less experienced CSOs along with larger, well experienced CSOs in presenting relevant and viable project proposals guided by broad terms of reference. This approach worked to level the playing field making it possible for both smaller and larger CSOs to compete mainly on the merits of their proposed project scope and interventions and demonstrated institutional capacity particularly in COVID-19 response.

Interested CSOs were guided in preparing their project concepts through a webinar, access to key project documents and information materials, and an interactive platform for frequently asked questions. The submitted project concepts (more than 100 were received) were evaluated based on criteria that were notified during the call.

Following the evaluation of the concepts, short lists of CSOs were presented and deliberated with country offices that then resulted in the preselection of 10 CSOs from target regions and countries that will implement activities under the TA.

The pre-selected CSOs will be engaged through direct contracting (or single-source selection) and in preparation for this, the TA is supporting the CSOs to register in ADB's CMS and to further enhance their project proposals vis-à-vis the TA scope and outputs. The CSOs are also being supported to navigate ADB's procurement system by preparing them on what to expect during the request for proposal and the ensuing contract negotiation stages, and sharing the standard templates for simplified technical and financial proposals in advance so they know what to expect and have enough time to prepare once the request for proposal is issued.

---

[99] ADB. Mitigating the Impact of COVID-19 through Community-Led Interventions.

BOX 20

Under the JFPR-funded TA, Mitigating the Impact of COVID-19 through Community-Led Interventions,[a] ADB used a two-stage process for identifying and procurement CSOs to support community-led interventions to respond to COVID-19. Under the first stage, in December 2020, NGOC held a webinar to let CSOs know about the call for project concepts (over 500 CSOs registered and more than 200 participated); and provided templates and guidelines for CSOs to prepare a project concept. ADB accepted project concepts until January 2021. The project team then short listed the project concepts and began the due diligence process. They also worked closely with the resident missions to select the project concepts that would best align with ADB's COVID-19 response (one of the criteria). Finally, the project team used direct contracting to engage each of the selected CSOs.

ADB = Asian Development Bank, COVID-19 = coronavirus disease, CSO = civil society organization, JFPR = Japan Fund for Prosperous and Resilient Asia and the Pacific, NGOC = NGO and Civil Society Center, TA = technical assistance.
[a] ADB. Mitigating the Impact of COVID-19 through Community-Led Interventions.
Source: Asian Development Bank.

Tips and guidance:
(i) Provide guidance and information to prospective CSOs through as many channels as possible: e.g., webinar, interactive Q&A platform, online, via e-mail.
(ii) Advertise the opportunity widely, including through social media (LinkedIn, Facebook, Twitter, WeChat, Telegram, Instagram), utilizing the social media platforms that will best reach the target audience
(iii) Ask peak CSO networks or umbrella CSO bodies in the target DMCs to promote the opportunity to their member CSOs, particularly smaller and local CSOs.
(iv) Ensure the first stage of calls for concepts is simple enough for local CSOs to apply, but require enough detail for the evaluation committee to make a fair assessment.
(v) Ensure there are broad terms of reference to allow CSOs as much flexibility as possible in proposing innovative and promising solutions.
(vi) Scope CSOs that are likely to apply and determine whether they have the existing skill set(s) to apply for the assignment; if not, build (and budget for) capacity-building support into the second stage (to assist these CSOs apply through CMS).
(vii) Detail in the PAM the mechanism and process, including participation of local community and/or CSOs.

In summary, consider the following for use of innovative approaches for procuring CSOs:
(i) Use these approaches when wanting to attract **innovative proposals from CSOs** on how to deal with a specific development issue. This is a fundamentally different approach from ADB or DMC governments deciding on their preferred solution to a development problem and seeking expressions of interest from firms to implement that preferred solution. All three approaches presented in this section allow the CSO to *propose* a solution, and then ADB or the DMC government can select from among the proposed solutions.
(ii) Use these approaches when **multiple solutions are required** to address a development problem. The approaches described in this section are suitable when a range of solutions are required, not just a single solution.
(iii) Use these approaches when both ADB and the DMC implementing agency are aware of and **committed to the extra time and effort required**. Innovation often takes extra time and effort to implement the proposed approaches, and the project team needs to be committed to this.

(iv)   Use these approaches when **DMC capacity can support CSOs** to implement the proposed solutions. In some situations (e.g., FCAS), some of these innovative approaches may not be suitable for this reason: the government may not have the capacity to support the CSO-proposed initiative.

Partnerships between ADB and Civil Society Organizations

As a convenor of partnerships, ADB will promote dialogue and collaboration among a diverse range of partners in the region, including CSOs.

While consulting services and nonconsulting services provide remuneration to service providers, partnerships recognize the contribution and resources that the partners jointly provide in the form of finance, risk-sharing capacity, or in-kind contributions toward common development objectives. Four modalities allow ADB to form partnerships with CSOs: (i) knowledge partnerships; (ii) development partnerships, either ADB-wide cooperation arrangements for development partnerships or cooperation arrangements specific to a country, region, sector, or theme; (iii) affiliation agreements; and (iv) financing partnerships.

Integrity due diligence must be performed in accordance with the guidelines and instructions for each type of partnership.

For more information on ADB partnerships, ADB staff can visit ADB's Knowledge Partnership Toolbox. The Knowledge Partnerships Toolbox provides ADB staff with detailed information and guidance on partnerships and the processes that must be followed.

Knowledge Partnerships

A knowledge partnership, which is established through a knowledge partnership agreement (KPA), is appropriate when a CSO knowledge partner has a common knowledge objective with ADB and is an equal partner in the development of the knowledge output. ADB and the CSO jointly develop and agree on the objectives and outputs of the knowledge partnership. Under a KPA, ADB shares part of the cost of the knowledge output. KPAs fall outside the scope of the Procurement Policy, i.e., it falls outside the scope of the *Guidelines on the Use of Consultants* (2013, as amended from time to time) and, therefore, have several eligibility criteria and require two approvals from the initiating department's vice president. Staff intending to use or explore the instrument are recommended to engage early in the process with their TA counsel and the designated procurement officer. Staff may also consult the Strategy, Policy, and Partnerships Department (Strategic Partnerships Division) for clarifications.

Knowledge partnerships are associations and networks of individuals or organizations with common objectives and whose members collaborate and contribute knowledge, experience, resources, and networks. Knowledge partnerships usually require a strategic, structural, and cultural fit between the knowledge partners, which engage in joint decision-making and action in a collaborative process.[100] In a knowledge partnership, the objectives are jointly agreed upon, and specific outputs are jointly developed by ADB and the knowledge partner.[101]

---

[100] ADB. 2011. *Guidelines for Knowledge Partnerships*. Manila.
[101] ADB. Knowledge Partnerships.

Where a CSO is engaged as a knowledge partner and there is payment[102] to the knowledge partner under TA Operations, staff must complete the process in accordance with the relevant guidance, including the How to Guide.[103]

Development partnerships

Civil society organizations as development partners. ADB will partner with a diverse range of organizations, including CSOs, to address the risks and challenges in the region, and to complement its core activities through sharing knowledge and expertise.[104] Development partnerships with CSOs may either be ADB-wide or specific to a country, region, sector, or theme. The features of development partnerships (both ADB-wide and specific) are that they: (i) typically, do not raise issues involving ADB policy considerations; (ii) do not exclusively serve to mobilize financing; and (iii) do not involve any payments or the transfer of funds between ADB and the development partner.

Cooperation arrangements for ADB-wide development partnerships. In addition to the criteria identified in the para. above, ADB-wide cooperation arrangements for development partnerships are usually high-level, involve more than one department or office, support ADB's corporate strategy, and are usually managed by the Strategy, Policy, and Partnerships Department.

Cooperation arrangements for specific development partnerships. In addition to the criteria identified in two paras. above, development partnerships under specific cooperation arrangements have the following features: (i) they involve development partnership activities limited by scope, by region, by country, by sector, or by theme; (ii) they typically involve only one department or office, or two or more departments or offices reporting to the same vice president; and (iii) are managed by the interested office or department.

Affiliation agreements with civil society organizations

ADB's acquisition of observer or member status in forums, networks, or initiatives is referred to as affiliation. Affiliation is separate and distinct from knowledge partnership agreements, cooperation arrangements (where there is no transfer of funds), and consulting services.

Formal affiliations define relationships with a specific organization, may or may not involve transfer of funds, and formalizes the basis of the relationship and affiliation. It may facilitate participation in external groups and think tanks, or enable participation as an observer or member in other organizations. This modality facilitates the exchange of ideas or information with various platforms or initiatives. ADB affiliations are always at a corporate level. Examples of such affiliations with CSOs is in Box 21.

---

[102] Generally, no more than $100,000 per year, unless justified: para. 15 (iii) Business Processes for Knowledge Partnerships under TA Operations.
[103] ADB. 2021. Knowledge Partnerships How-to Guide. Manila.
[104] ADB. 2017. Development Partnerships. *Operations Manual*. OM E3. Manila.

ADB has several affiliations with CSOs, including an affiliation with the International Initiative for Impact Evaluation (3ie). 3ie is a global membership organization, which funds, produces, quality assures, and synthesizes rigorous evidence. Another example is ADB's affiliation with the Toilet Board Coalition, a business-led membership organization, to scale market-based solutions to universal access to sanitation.

ADB's affiliations with CSO networks and initiatives are listed in ADB's Knowledge Partnership Toolbox, which is available to ADB staff, by searching for "affiliations."

ADB = Asian Development Bank, CSO = civil society organization.
Source: Asian Development Bank.

Civil society organizations as cofinanciers

ADB partners with a range of development partners, including bilateral arrangements, partnerships with the private sector, and partnerships with CSOs. This can be through project specific cofinancing, financing partnership facilities, single- and multi-donor trust funds, and framework cofinancing arrangements. ADB will expand partnerships with philanthropic CSOs to develop innovative funding arrangements for ADB operations.[105] Under sovereign cofinancing, regional departments can use any source of funds as cofinanciers, including concessional sources, such as funds provided by nonprofit foundations.

An example of cofinancing is the Bill and Melinda Gates Foundation, which has contributed $3.5 million in cumulative project specific cofinancing, and $19 million in trust fund contributions (including $3 million to the Sanitation Financing Partnership Trust Fund, under the Water Financing Partnership Facility).[106]

Parallel financing from civil society organizations for ADB-financed projects. For parallel financing, ADB and its financing partners each finance specific, identifiable contract packages and this can be done on tied or untied terms. When ADB and a CSO agree for the terms to be tied, the financing CSO partner implements and administers their assigned components, including administering its own CSO funds, in parallel with the ADB-financed components. In this situation, ADB and the financing CSO partner each use its own procurement, disbursement, and other policies and procedures; and impose no legal obligations on each other. ADB and the financing partner closely coordinate during the processing and implementation of the project. When the terms are untied, the financing can be administered by ADB, and ADB's policies and procedures apply. Parallel financing may be fully or partially administered by ADB, or not at all.

---

105 ADB. 2020. Financing Partnerships. *Operations Manual*. OM E1. Manila.
106 ADB. Financing Partners: Bill & Melinda Gates Foundation.

5

Other Considerations for Civil Society Organization Engagement

Other Ways to Engage with Civil Society Organizations

Fragile and conflict-affected situations

Asian Development Bank (ADB) will strengthen collaborations with civil society organizations (CSOs) in fragile and conflict-affected situations (FCAS) to make ADB operations fragility- and conflict-sensitive.[107] CSOs may play a more prominent role in FCAS. When societal links are weak, CSOs can help build connections between people and communities and among governments, aid agencies, and development partners. When public services are disrupted, CSOs may become providers of basic social services and support social cohesion. CSOs facilitate stronger governance by creating partnerships between community groups and local governments. They may introduce participatory approaches to community-level decision-making, supporting women, youth, and other vulnerable groups, strengthen their position and voice by creating safe spaces for dialogue. As such, CSOs can play a stabilizing role, facilitate dialogue, and create networks and access in otherwise difficult to reach or dangerous areas. In doing so, CSOs identify and respond to local drivers of fragility and conflict.

The FCAS and Small Island Developing States (SIDS) Approach outlines an operational approach for ADB to improve development effectiveness in FCAS and SIDS.[108] Through the approach, ADB will apply tailored processes and procedures to operations in FCAS and SIDS with the goal of improving project results—and ultimately improving livelihoods in these countries. The FCAS and SIDS Approach recommends expanded consultations with CSOs and CSO participation at country and project level.

CSOs play an active role in supporting the CPS process in FCAS by helping conduct community consultations part of the fragility and resilience assessments (FRA) and contributing to the CPS preparation to improve country-level understanding and the contextual risks. The FRA analyzes the causes of fragility, and proposes actions to manage the fragility and vulnerability, and to build resilience.

---

[107] Footnote 3, para. 26.
[108] ADB. 2021. *Fragile and Conflict-Affected Situations and Small Island Developing States Approach.* Manila

BOX 22

Prior to the government change in mid-August 2021, the Asian Development Bank undertook a fragility and resilience assessment (FRA) in Afghanistan.[a] The overall objective of the FRA was to inform the formulation of the then-upcoming-Afghanistan CPS through a better understanding of how ADB can best operate and deliver results in such a complex and changing environment.

The FRA adopted a fully participatory and inclusive approach, including consultations with government agencies, development partners, civil society, and Afghan communities. ADB engaged a local CSO to carry out extensive consultation in five regional capitals. The CSO employed a mixed-method (quantitative and qualitative) approach involving surveys, key informant interviews, and focus group discussions to capture public perceptions about the drivers and underlying causes of fragility and resilience in both rural and urban areas of Afghanistan. More than 480 people—45% of them women—participated, and in each community, residents from a wide range of socioeconomic profiles joined.

In recruiting the service provider, ADB requested a methodology to ensure an inclusive approach to the population in terms of ethnicity, culture, and gender; and include an equally representative and inclusive team to access targeted areas and populations.

ADB = Asian Development Bank, CPS = country partnership strategy, CSO = civil society organization, FCAS = fragile and conflict-affected situations.
[a] ADB maintains the hold it placed on its assistance in Afghanistan effective 15 August 2021.
Source: Asian Development Bank.

Focusing on the need to coherently address people's vulnerability before, during, and after a crisis or protected crises in FCAS and disaster emergency situations, in line with Asian Development Fund 13 commitments, the FCAS and SIDS Approach supports the humanitarian development peace nexus.[109] The humanitarian development peace nexus, or triple nexus, was developed in response to calls made by humanitarian, development, and peace actors for enhanced policy and operational coherence. It provides a clear framework, particularly in fragile and conflict-affected situations, to implement collaborative and complementary humanitarian and peace actions. In implanting the triple nexus, ADB and developing member countries (DMCs) will be brokering and building new or strengthening partnerships with CSOs, enhancing coherence and complementarity among development partners. Each actor remaining in its "sphere" of intervention and building on its comparative advantage.

In FCAS, meaningful CSO engagement will be undertaken in formal and informal contexts. Strengthening FCAS engagement with civil society forums, including women's and vulnerable groups, will involve in-country establishment of ADB–CSO consultative groups and platforms, including youth-led engagement mechanisms. Active and inclusive CSOs' participation will take place, not only during the development of FRAs and CPS

---

[109] Under Asian Development Fund 13, ADB will identify opportunities for humanitarian-peace-development nexus aspects (the Triple Nexus), in line with ADB's value addition, especially in fragile countries and by working on the fragility to stability continuum. ADB. 2020. *Asian Development Fund 13 Donors' Report.* Manila. para. 39.

preparation, but also through consultation during project processing. This engagement is essential, especially in conflict contexts where it is key that the CPS and the derived projects integrate the views of all the beneficiaries.

As described in section 2, in complex environments, where security and conflict risks and distance are an issue, CSOs may be engaged as independent third-party monitoring.

Disaster and emergency situations

CSO engagement can have an important role in ADB-financed operations, especially in disaster risk management and emergency response. ADB will cooperate with key stakeholders, including CSOs, on sustainable financing of disaster risk reduction (DRR).[110]

CSO engagement can have an important role to address various aspects of risk management. Many types of organizations must work together to reduce risk and prepare for, respond to, and recover from disasters and emergencies. Building on its comparative advantage, ADB will seek to strengthen collaboration, coherence, and complementarity with other organizations. National and local CSOs are particularly important partners in achieving greater community resilience.

Under the disaster response facility, ADB will bring in CSOs in response operations where relevant in concessional lending.[111] ADB may partner with CSOs after a disaster to reestablish basic services and rebuild critical infrastructure at the community level. To leverage its assistance in emergency situations, the contribution of CSOs in disaster response will be counted toward the counterpart requirements for ADB loans.[112]

Key phases of disaster where CSO engagement is typically high are as follows:
- (i) Disaster:
  - ➲ CSOs act as first frontline rescue responders, emergency support (food, shelter, health) services.
  - ➲ CSOs engage in initial coordination, communications, and response management with the United Nations and governments.

- (ii) Emergency response or transition phase (partnering with specialized [relief] agencies):
  - ➲ Rehabilitate high priority physical and social infrastructure, revitalize basic services, and jump-start economic productivity.
  - ➲ After the emergency crisis period, shift to transitional social, institutional, and capacity requirements, including social and economic reintegration.

- (iii) Recovery phase:
  - ➲ Conduct joint damage and needs assessment with relevant partners.
  - ➲ Provide emergency short-term transitional assistance.
  - ➲ Plan and design comprehensive rehabilitation and reconstruction programs.[113]

---

[110] ADB. 2015. Disaster and Emergency Assistance. *Operations Manual*. OM D7. Manila.
[111] ADB. 2020. *Concessional Assistance Policy for the ADF 13 Period: Policy Paper*. Manila.
[112] ADB. 2020. *Concessional Assistance Policy for the ADF 13 Period: Policy Paper*. Manila. ADB. 2015. Disaster and Emergency Assistance. *Operations Manual*. OM D7. Manila.
[113] Footnote 110.

BOX 23

The 2021 Revised Disaster and Emergency Assistance Policy (RDEAP) provides an updated policy framework to enhance strategic guidance for ADB's assistance for disasters and emergencies, covering geophysical hazard events (such as earthquakes, tsunamis, and volcanic eruptions), extreme weather hazard events (such as droughts, floods, and tropical cyclones), as well as situations related to food, health, biological, industrial, and technological events, and post-conflict situations. It draws from a review of the 2004 policy that recognized CSOs are well placed to implement community-focused components contained in many emergency assistance loan (EAL) projects.[a]

The updated policy covers risk reduction, preparedness, and response. It seeks to support DMCs to strengthen resilience to disasters and emergencies, including the enhanced management of residual risk. Its scope reflects ADB's development mandate, complementing humanitarian assistance and peace-building activities.[b]

The RDEAP rests on four underlying principles:
  (i)   stressing that risk management begins with risk reduction;
  (ii)   recognizing disaster and emergency risk management as an integral part of the development process;
  (iii) acknowledging that DMCs have differentiated risk profiles and, thus, opportunities for enhanced resilience; and
  (iv)   emphasizing that timely, carefully planned, and well-designed relief, early recovery, and reconstruction interventions and solutions reduce the near- and longer-term social, institutional, and economic impacts of disasters and emergencies, and facilitate resilient recovery.

Building on its comparative advantage, ADB will seek to strengthen collaboration, coherence, and complementarity with other organizations, and build partnerships and coordinate with CSOs, among other stakeholders, to address various aspects of risk management and build greater community resilience.

ADB will apply participatory processes as an integral part of its disaster and emergency assistance. It recognizes the importance of CSO participation and of taking into account diverse perspectives and contributions of all segments of society, including women, children and youth, older persons, and marginalized groups, and the specific contexts and needs of individual communities, including in project design and implementation and related decision-making processes.

ADB = Asian Development Bank, CSO = civil society organization, DEAP = disaster and emergency assistance policy (2004), DMC = developing member country, EAL = emergency assistance loan, RDEAP = Revised Disaster and Emergency Assistance Policy (2021).
[a] ADB. 2019. *Review of the 2004 Disaster and Emergency Assistance Policy*. Manila.
[b] ADB. 2021. Revised Disaster and Emergency Assistance Policy. Manila.
Source: Asian Development Bank.

Across all aspects of disaster response and recovery, good communications and the inclusion and active participation of local communities is encouraged to ensure their voices are heard.

See the Climate Change and Disaster Risk Management webpage for more information.

Engaging civil society organizations in resident missions and representative offices

Under ADB's Resident Mission Policy, the resident mission provides the primary operational interface between ADB and the host DMC. It strives to maximize the efficiency, effectiveness, and impact of ADB operations in the DMC. To fulfill the client orientation approach set out in the policy, resident mission staff should understand the DMC's society and culture and establish long-term engagement with CSOs. One of the two objectives of the policy is to create strong partnerships with DMC development stakeholders, including CSOs. Therefore, resident missions must lead in and include civil society relations as part of their work.[114]

The CSO Cooperation Network includes a CSO anchor from each resident mission who supports and provides coordination of the office's outreach with CSOs. The resident mission anchor works with operations staff, sector and thematic groups, and the NGO and Civil Society Center (NGOC), as appropriate. ADB staff may find working with umbrella or peak CSO groups or CSO networks is an effective entry point for CSO engagement by a resident mission. Civil society advisory groups—groups of key civil society representatives established to help staff stay abreast of civil society activity—may be another useful entry point for CSO engagement.

The CSO anchor's roles (either at headquarters or in the resident mission) may include the following:
- (i) Building and strengthening communications with CSOs, reaching out to and meeting with CSOs and networks.
- (ii) Maintaining a database of CSOs and their activities, issues, and concerns active in country and operating in areas and/or sectors relevant to ADB's portfolio.
- (iii) Providing support to the operations of the NGOC and the ADB-wide CSO Cooperation Network, by sharing knowledge and expertise in CSO engagement.
- (iv) Providing operational support to increase CSO engagement in ADB operations, such as sharing with ADB information about CSOs' priority issues; geographical coverage; sector presence, expertise, and concerns in country.
- (v) Support and coordinate the CSO advisory group, if convened.
- (vi) Improving design methodologies for CSO engagement, including preparing a consultation and participation plan for the resident mission, and taking charge of its implementation.
- (vii) Providing guidance to the Country Director, NGOC, relevant regional department, mission leaders, and offices on activities related to methodological design and analysis related to CSOs.

An annotated terms of reference (TOR) for a CSO anchor or focal point at the resident mission level is in Appendix 4.

Pilot activities

ADB may wish to test the innovative approaches CSOs develop for possible use in ADB-financed projects. Pilot testing of project approaches is allowed under various modalities, as described in Operations Manual Technical Assistance (OM D12 SI Attachment 1), Project Readiness Financing (OM D16), and Small Expenditure Financing Facility (OM D17).[115]

An example of a pilot program involving CSOs is in Box 24.

---

[114] ADB. 2000. *Resident Mission Policy*. Manila.
[115] ADB. 2019. Small Expenditure Financing Facility. *Operations Manual*. OM D17. Manila.

> **BOX 24**
>
> **Kathmandu's Youth-Led Approaches to Sustainable Bagmati River Improvement (Pilot and Demonstration).** Supporting the Sustainable Bagmati River Basin Management Program, the youth-led PDA virtually trained 1,703 World's Largest Lesson participants (ages 13–24) through a 90-minute interactive module. Another 196 participants underwent a more intensive 6-week training (ages 18–29) about the SDGs and 3R (reuse, reduce, and recycle) principles using intersector and intergenerational approaches. There were 107 locally trained youth facilitators and 10 SDGs training youth facilitators who implemented the training from August to November 2020. As a part of the SDGs training, more than 30 young people joined a virtual dialogue with officials from the Government of Nepal, NGOs, CBOs, and/or activists, and local politicians to discover new pathways to make the river healthy and clean by strengthening ongoing initiatives and developing new collaborative spaces. By the end of the program, 32 youth-led project proposals were presented, of which 19 proposals proceeded to project implementation and were further incorporated into ward, school, and CSO plans. The PDA demonstrated strong evidence of the value of engaging with young people in the SDGs and their effectiveness in building inclusive, sustainable, and climate change-resilient behaviors in local youth communities. The PDA recommended to replicate and upscale such youth-led programs and to continue the meaningful engagement of youth in taking actions to contribute to Agenda 2030 and the achievement of the SDGs.
>
> ---
>
> CBO = community-based organization, NGO = nongovernment organization, PDA = pilot and demonstration activity, SDG = Sustainable Development Goal.
> Source: ADB. 2021. *Highlights of ADB's Cooperation with Civil Society Organizations 2020.* Manila.

Nonsovereign operations

As the project cycle, business process, and financing modalities for nonsovereign operations (NSOs) differ from sovereign operations, the opportunities for CSO engagement in NSOs is also different. However, engagement with CSOs in NSOs is generally the same as sovereign operations in the following aspects of infrastructure operations: (i) designing a project that incorporates CSO engagement, and (ii) implementing and monitoring a project with CSO engagement.

NSOs focus on private sector projects, operate in a commercial environment, and (in some cases) provide financing to private clients involved in private–public partnerships. CSOs may also be borrowers or clients, particularly when ADB provides financing to financial intermediaries. Project timelines are compressed compared with sovereign operations, and ADB's involvement often comes later in project development. Nevertheless, CSOs are key project stakeholders, and their feedback is sought through a meaningful consultation process. CSOs also provide feedback on project safeguards performance, particularly through a project's grievance redress mechanism. On higher risk or sensitive projects, ADB and the client will seek to engage with CSOs during the due diligence process.

In select cases—usually for large, complex projects—CSOs may work with the client and communities. ADB does not procure the services of CSOs in these cases, but may facilitate the development of partnerships with CSOs, including procurement of services of CSOs by the client, to increase transparency and trust with external stakeholders. CSOs may be interviewed on extended annual review report missions to gain insights into the project's developments.[116]

---

[116] ADB. 2018. Extended Annual Review Reports for Nonsovereign Operations. *Project Administration Instructions.* PAI 6.07B. Manila.

On sensitive projects, ADB may work with the client to assist the client in procuring specialized services from CSOs to implement safeguards management plans (e.g., indigenous people's plans, environmental management plans, involuntary resettlement plans, and gender action plans [GAPs]) or monitor the implementation of such plans for a particular project.

Examples of CSOs engaged in NSOs are presented in Box 25.

BOX 25

Working with Himalayan Wildlife Foundation for Biodiversity Action Plan Implementation under the Gulpur Hydropower Project[a]

The section of the Poonch River where the 102 megawatt Gulpur Hydropower Plant Project (GHPP) is located was declared a national park in December 2010 by the local authorities due to the presence of the Kashmir Catfish (*Glyptothorax kashmirensis*), listed as critically endangered; and the Mahseer (*Tor putitora*), listed as endangered in the IUCN Red List. A critical habitat assessment confirmed that the project is sited in a critical habitat; therefore, a biodiversity action plan (BAP) was developed to achieve overall net gain for both fish species and conservation of the national park. Mira Power Ltd. (MPL), the GHPP developer, in consultation with the government's Fisheries and Wildlife Department, selected and contracted the Himalayan Wildlife Foundation (HWF) as the implementation organization required for BAP implementation.

HWF, a nonprofit organization, demonstrated its expertise, experience, interest, and willingness to perform biodiversity protection in the national park for delivery of technical services and materials required for BAP implementation. HWF entered into a contract agreement with MPL in April 2016 to fulfill the following scope and services: (i) hire and manage the staff for protection activities; (ii) procure and maintain equipment and materials required for supporting the watch and ward team; (iii) collect data and prepare reports on watch and ward and management of sediment mining, illegal hunting, and illegal fishing activities, violations, and others; (iv) prepare and submit the reports to present findings and recommendations to the Management Committee and the Monitoring and Evaluation (M&E) consultant; (v) provide training to the staff of the Fisheries and Wildlife Department in protection and management of national park and wildlife; (vi) oversee the operation of the Mahaseer hatchery at Moli Nullah and release fish into the river, and provide further technical advice and support where needed; (vii) maintain contact with local communities and stakeholders and promote awareness on biodiversity protection among them; and (viii) advise the Management Committee and the M&E consultant on ways and means of improving the effectiveness of the BAP. The quarterly monitoring reported positive changes in the communities, including (i) increased awareness of licensed fishers to call, inform and notify HWF about illegal fishing activities in the river; (ii) local angler support to watch and ward staff should arguments or scuffles arise with illegal fishers; and (iii) visiting anglers' appreciation for the fishing opportunity to fish in the Poonch River recognizing its unique attributes.

continued on next page

Box 25 continued

Working with CSO as Service Providers to Implement a Biodiversity Offset Program Under the Indonesia Sarulla Geothermal Power Project[b]
In 2013, ADB provided funding to support the development, construction, operation, and maintenance of three geothermal power generation units with a total capacity of about 320 megawatts in Indonesia. The environmental impact assessment determined that an offset program was required to achieve a no net loss or net gain in biodiversity in accordance with ADB's SPS. Through extensive consultation with project stakeholders, including government officials, communities, CSOs, and subject matter experts, an offset area was identified and a Biodiversity Offset Management Plan (BOMP) was developed and agreed upon in 2020. The key mechanism for the BOMP's implementation is a Community Conservation Agreement between community stakeholders and a CSO service provider. The borrower worked with ADB to develop the scope of work and select a CSO service provider who had the experience, capacity, and technical capability to implement the BOMP. The Sumatra Rainforest Institute, the selected CSO, was contracted by the borrower in 2021 and the implementation of the BOMP has commenced.

ADB = Asian Development Bank, CSO = civil society organization, IUCN = International Union for Conservation of Nature, SPS = Safeguard Policy Statement.
[a]   ADB. Pakistan: Gulpur Hydropower Project.
[b]   ADB. Indonesia. Sarulla Geothermal Power Project.
Source: Asian Development Bank.

Good governance

CSOs offer an additional and complementary means of channeling the energies of private citizens. CSOs can be helpful in identifying people's interests, mobilizing public opinion in support of these interests, and organizing action accordingly. They can provide governments with a useful ally in enhancing participation in communities and fostering a bottom-up approach to economic and social development.[117] CSOs can help promote good governance and improve accountability of ADB-financed projects through monitoring.

According to the Strategy 2030 Operational Plan for Priority 6 Strengthening Governance and Institutional Capacity 2019–2024, ADB will explore opportunities to increase citizen engagement in designing, implementing, and monitoring ADB operations, including streamlining grants and partnership mechanisms. ADB will work in partnership with a broad range of CSOs to strengthen social accountability and improve service delivery, particularly through digital technology which promotes citizen engagement in government service delivery. ADB will work with youth organizations, smaller CSOs, and networks of CSOs, who draw together the perspectives of grassroots CSOs, to better engage with citizens for improved governance. ADB's membership in the Open Government Partnership (OGP) is an example of how ADB encourages governments and CSOs to collaborate for improved governance and accountability. The NGOC will share knowledge on how to successfully engage citizens and CSOs in projects for improved governance and responsiveness to the needs of citizens.[118]

ADB has been a member of the OGP since 2014 and is one of OGP's eight multilateral partners.[119] OGP, established in 2011, is a member-based organization working with national and subnational organizations on transforming how

---

[117]   Footnote 41.
[118]   Footnote 23.
[119]   Open Government Partnership. Multilateral Organizations.

government serves its citizens. OGP and ADB cooperate on knowledge events and programs, and several DMCs are also members of OGP. Biannually, each member country must submit an action plan to OGP that is created with CSOs to identify specific and concrete commitments that country will take to enhance transparency, accountability, and public participation in government.[120]

According to the Operational Plan for Priority 6, ADB will identify and introduce digital technology to enable CSO participation in the national budget processes, including advancing women's participation in the budgeting process. Greater transparency with civil society and other stakeholders, including on terms of financing and official support, will help ensure equal footing in the procurement process.[121]

See the Governance webpage for more information on the Sustainable Development and Climate Change Department, Governance Thematic Group.

Anticorruption

Under Strategy 2030 Operational Plan for Priority 6, ADB will promote its zero-tolerance policy toward corruption and work with civil society to support anticorruption efforts. ADB will empower CSOs to help fight corruption.[122]

ADB will consider working with local and international CSOs to support regional anticorruption efforts. CSOs, such as chambers of commerce, can participate in government–business councils to provide feedback to DMCs on governance and anticorruption issues. ADB will support training, education, and dissemination activities for civil society, governments, and other stakeholders to reduce corruption in the region.[123] CSO monitoring is used to enhance accountability and anticorruption efforts. If the CSO engagement is not covered by other applicable policies and guidance material, staff should consult OAI for any integrity due diligence, conflict of interest, or other integrity-related requirements. See the Anticorruption and Integrity webpage for more information on OAI.

Accountability Mechanism

ADB's Accountability Mechanism provides a forum for those adversely affected by ADB-financed projects to seek solutions to their problems, and to report noncompliance with ADB's policies and procedures. CSOs may be representatives of project-affected people who are complainants on ADB-financed projects. CSOs are eligible to file complaints under the Accountability Mechanism; these CSOs must provide appropriate evidence to represent project-affected people. ADB also conducts regular outreach and dissemination activities on the Accountability Mechanism with civil society. ADB may also contract CSOs to conduct outreach on the mechanism.[124]

The Accountability Mechanism has two complementary functions: (i) a problem-solving function to respond to specific complaints through a range of informal methods; and (ii) a compliance review function to investigate alleged violations of ADB's operational policies and procedures that have resulted in or are likely to cause direct and material harm. CSOs may be useful as facilitators and by providing insights into causes and possible solutions.

See the Accountability Mechanism webpage for more information.

---

[120] Open Government Partnership. Members.
[121] Footnote 23.
[122] Footnote 23.
[123] ADB. 1998. *Anticorruption: Our Framework Policies and Strategies*. Manila.
[124] ADB. 2012. Accountability Mechanism. *Operations Manual*. OM L1. Manila.

Access to information

ADB's inclusive communications strategies, which ensure public access to information and two-way exchange of information, help CSOs engage in the development process. The objective of ADB's Access to Information Policy (AIP) is to promote stakeholder trust in ADB and to increase the development impact of ADB. The principles of the policy include the clear, timely, and appropriate disclosure of information about ADB operations to stakeholders to build stakeholders' capacity to meaningfully engage with ADB. Civil society is one of the key stakeholders under the AIP.

The AIP reflects ADB's commitment to transparency, accountability, and participation by stakeholders in ADB-supported development activities. It also recognizes the right of people to seek, receive, and give information about ADB's operations. The policy applies to documents and information that ADB produces, requires to be produced by its borrowers or clients, or are produced and provided to ADB by other parties during ADB operations. The AIP will be implemented in accordance with arrangements approved by ADB management and documents and information will be made publicly available in accordance with ADB's normal procedures.

The AIP and associated OM L3 provide detailed guidance on the principles of the policy and the steps staff must take to provide information to key stakeholders, including civil society.

More information is found in the AIP.[125]

Country safeguard systems and related feedback mechanisms

CSOs are involved in the consultations around country safeguard systems and strengthening their use in ADB-financed projects. Once draft equivalence and acceptability assessments (including gap-filling measures, if any) at the national, subnational, sector, or agency level are prepared, they will be documented and disclosed and ADB will organize in-country consultation workshops to solicit comments and feedback from stakeholders, including from civil society.[126]

Civil society organizations and localizing the Sustainable Development Goals

CSOs have a key role in assisting ADB and DMC governments in localizing the SDGs. CSOs can promote awareness of the SGDs at a local level and assist local governments with design and implementation of interventions to support progress toward achieving the SDGs. They play an important role in monitoring SDG implementation at the local level, and may campaign for greater focus on the SDGs, particularly when acting in their advocacy roles.

Civil society organizations' engagement in knowledge products and services

ADB shares knowledge generated by CSOs, with CSOs, and through CSOs. Knowledge products and events may be part of ADB-financed projects, TAs, institutional events, such as the annual meeting (see below), and collaboration with other stakeholders. The relevant business processes apply to the engagement of CSOs as resource persons, service providers, and consultants (see section 4 for more details).

---

[125] ADB. 2018. *Access to Information Policy*. Manila.
[126] ADB. 2013. Safeguard Policy Statement. *Operations Manual*. OM F1. Manila.

Civil society organizations as a conduit for citizen engagement

Working with CSOs is one mechanism to effectively access the views of citizens through organizations that represent specific groups of citizens, and through CSO competence in promoting government transparency and accountability. Citizen engagement is core to better development results and ADB's Strategy 2030 Operational Priority 6, Strengthening Governance and Institutional Capacity, incorporates a commitment to enhancing citizen engagement in ADB operations to improve the quality and relevance of public services in DMCs. It states:

> ADB will work more closely with civil society and citizen networks to ensure accountability, transparency, and inclusivity. Meaningful citizen engagement and governance and institutional capacity efforts are critical because they help determine whether well-intentioned policies lead to desired development outcomes and meet citizen expectations.[127]

The corporate results framework includes a level 2A indicator: "Citizen Engagement Mechanisms Adopted (number)." Multiple entry points exist for citizen engagement across ADB, and CSOs act as intermediaries to accessing the views of citizens. There are opportunities to capitalize on opportunities in the policy sphere, for example, through commitments in policy and results-based lending, to encourage citizen engagement in governance, including through innovative approaches to citizen-led monitoring and accountability.

BOX 26

The design of the proposed Khyber Pakhtunkhwa Cities Improvement Project (KPCIP)[a] in Abbottabad, Pakistan will incorporate lessons and inputs from a UCCRTF-financed TA,[b] which is implemented by Oxfam and its local CSO partner, Omar Ashgar Khan Development Foundation. The KPCIP loan will pilot citizens' engagement and community education on effective waste reduction and solid waste management. The community-led TA project is focused on micro-level community-based improvement of solid waste management services to fewer than 10,000 people. The CSOs' role in mobilizing community stakeholder groups, including community members representing different vulnerable groups, local authorities, and other relevant sectors, is important in building community ownership on the community-led TA project. The TA project complements the KPCIP, which is a citywide intervention on waste management covering almost half a million people. Lessons from the community-led TA project can help ADB gain understanding on how to motivate the community on gender justice mainstreaming, addressing the needs of waste pickers, the logistics of door-to-door collection, the need for water conservation and options for 3R waste reduction (reduce, reuse, recycle). The Omar Ashgar Khan Development Foundation serves as the link between the community-led TA project and the citizens with the bigger development KPCIP PRF and proposed loan project KPCIP to strengthen community resilience and ensure long-term impacts.

ADB = Asian Development Bank, CSO = civil society organization, PRF = project readiness financing, TA = technical assistance, UCCRTF = Urban Climate Change Resilience Trust Fund.
[a] ADB. Pakistan. Khyber Pakhtunkhwa Cities Improvement Projects - Project Readiness Financing.
[b] ADB. Regional: Promoting Urban Climate Change Resilience in Selected Asian Cities - Development of Pilot Activities and Project Development Support (Subproject 3).
Source: Oxfam.

---

127 Footnote 23.

Engaging with civil society organizations at ADB's Annual Meeting

ADB engages directly with CSOs at its annual meeting. ADB develops a civil society program each year as part of the annual meeting. In most years,[128] the ADB President (representing ADB senior management) meets with CSO representatives at the annual meeting, giving an opportunity for CSOs to raise questions for ADB management on topics relating to ADB's support to development across the Asia and Pacific region, along with ADB's engagement with CSOs. CSOs are accredited to attend the annual meeting each year, and in practice, this accreditation is "rolled over" into subsequent annual meetings, so that each CSO only must go through the accreditation process once. For more information on the accreditation process, review the report on *Fifty-Fourth Annual Meeting of the Board of Governors of the Asian Development Bank: Attendance of Civil Society Organizations.*[129]

Secondments from civil society organizations

Staff may be engaged through secondments from CSOs. In these circumstances, both ADB and the CSO recognize the benefit of placing a CSO staff member within ADB for a defined period and with a clear role and scope. Under this arrangement, ADB benefits from the CSO-centric knowledge that a CSO staff member brings, and the CSO benefits from their staff member gaining exposure to ADB processes and faculty.

Engaging Civil Society Organizations and Respecting Governments

The 2021 Operations Manual section E4, Promotion of Engagement with CSOs, notes that "ADB pursues an expanded program of engagement with CSOs, where appropriate, in its member countries, in consultation with the government, with a view to strengthen the effectiveness, sustainability, and quality of the development services ADB provides." It further states: "The fundamental relationship between ADB and a government, as well as the sovereignty of governments, continues to be recognized."[130]

ADB's contact with CSOs are a supplement to, and not a substitute for, government dialogue with citizen groups. Most countries have laws and regulations governing how CSOs operate, and it is important to understand these regulations before engaging. The setting of national development priorities and explaining them to the public (including explanations provided through CSOs) is the responsibility of the government concerned. Government–CSO relations vary greatly from country to country. In a few countries, some stakeholders view CSOs as oppositional and relations between the various development actors within a DMC may tend toward being adversarial. In other cases, local stakeholders, including governments and CSOs, may share similar goals and work closely with each other. In between are relationships between different stakeholders that are tolerant without being particularly supportive.

Given the diversity within the CSO sector, a government's relationship with any individual organization depends greatly on that organization's specific activities, purpose, ideology, and institutional or personal ties, all of which may vary over time. Governments are generally supportive of CSO involvement when CSOs can offer services

---

[128] This meeting between the ADB President and CSOs was not held at the 53rd Annual Meeting in 2020, due to COVID-19.
[129] ADB. 2020. *Fifty-Fourth Annual Meeting of the Board of Governors of the Asian Development Bank: Attendance of Civil Society Organizations.* Manila.
[130] Footnote 1.

that complement government activities. If a government objects to ADB's relationship with a CSO, staff members should explain the rationale for such contacts.

CSOs often believe that ADB can play the role of honest broker in bridging differences between the government and civil society. In cases in which a CSO proposes that ADB take an action that should rightfully be carried out by the government, ADB staff members should encourage the CSO to take its views and proposals to the relevant national authority, explaining that the fundamental relationship is between ADB and its member governments. Depending on the circumstances, it may be appropriate for staff members to facilitate dialogue between CSOs and governments, to assist in building bridges and promoting engagement.

In situations where a government is wary about ADB engaging with CSOs, staff members may consider notifying the government of meetings with CSOs that have been planned or inviting officials to arrange and participate in such discussions. However, in situations where CSOs are afraid of reprisals for sharing views, a CSO may wish to meet alone with ADB staff members. The lack of consultation during the selection process is often the source of difficulties that operational CSOs have in ADB-financed projects while working with governments, particularly local authorities.

Government officials are also sometimes concerned about the effectiveness of CSOs compared to private consultants operating within roles relating to project implementation. An Independent Evaluation Department study of CSO involvement in ADB operations determined that constraints on CSO involvement could have been reduced by (i) assessing the effectiveness of the legislative and regulatory environment for CSO involvement; (ii) examining the capacity of CSOs to engage in policy dialogue with the government; (iii) assessing the working arrangements that exist between the executing agency, CSOs, and ADB; and (iv) analyzing the institutional capacities, memberships, governance, and financial management systems of CSOs. Tensions between governments and CSOs could be reduced through capacity-building activities that ensure national and local governments can effectively manage CSO inputs. Such activities also tend to improve understanding among partners.[131]

Tips on addressing sensitivities concerning civil society organizations

(i) Highlight the benefits of broad participation and the potential contributions of CSOs to the national development strategy, and the roles that CSOs play in building relationships with and within communities.
(ii) Showcase specific examples of successful projects carried out with CSO support within the country.
(iii) Sensitively highlight the mechanisms for achieving positive multistakeholder–CSO collaboration in other DMCs.
(iv) Identify any stakeholder sensitivities about working with CSOs and try to resolve the concerns.
(v) Arrange meetings that bring together all relevant stakeholders, including ADB staff, government officials, and CSO representatives.
(vi) Encourage CSOs to strengthen their relationships with government agencies.
(vii) Interact with reputable CSOs that demonstrate high degree of integrity and place a high value on accountability.
(viii) Avoid CSOs that take an openly partisan stance or that play an active role in politics.
(ix) Celebrate when CSOs and government have jointly achieved effective development outcomes.

---

[131] ADB. 2006. *Special Evaluation Study of the Involvement of Civil Society Organizations in ADB Operations*. Manila.

Engaging with Advocacy Organizations

ADB recognizes the difference between development-oriented CSOs—such as service provider CSOs that may be involved in project design, delivery, and evaluation—and advocacy organizations. Advocacy organizations engage in policy dialogue and other means to influence the views, policies, and actions of governments and other organizations and stakeholders such as ADB, the media, and the community. ADB's engagement with advocacy organizations differs from its engagement with development CSOs, revolving primarily around policy dialogue. Some CSOs may do both advocacy and operational work, such as CSOs providing women refuges, but also advocating against gender-based violence.

Representatives of advocacy organizations deliver presentations at events such as civil society engagement training for project staff and civil society information sharing events, and they are often involved in ADB's annual meetings. Advocacy organizations often reach out to ADB to share concerns about projects or policies.

Civil society activists representing advocacy organizations or labor unions often ask for information about ADB-financed projects they monitor. Under the AIP, ADB commits to disclosing information in response to individual requests. In the case of people affected by ADB-financed projects, the AIP states that ADB will share information with them early enough to provide inputs into project design and implementation. All departments and offices are responsible for implementing the AIP. Staff members from operations departments play a key role in communicating with project stakeholders and making sure that disclosure requirements are met. Mission leaders should identify the necessary resources, including a budget that supports communication with affected peoples and CSOs (e.g., activities such as producing information materials in local language, and organizing workshops or events). Mission leaders are responsible for ensuring that people from the public, private, and nonprofit sectors with whom they interact are aware of the AIP and the public's right to access information from ADB. ADB does not selectively disclose information; all people have equal access to information that ADB makes available under the AIP. Notwithstanding staff obligations to respond to information requests and to monitor project communication activities to ensure compliance with the AIP, much of the responsibility for disclosing information about ADB-financed projects rests with the borrowing government or private sector sponsor.

Human rights defenders are often represented by civil society human rights advocacy groups. Examples include Human Rights Watch, Front Line Defenders, and FORUM-ASIA. Such groups and their local national member CSOs may engage with ADB over issues facing human rights defenders in the region. These groups may raise issues related to the work of human rights defenders, such as those who may raise issues around the treatment of activists (including civil society activists and journalists) who may face threats and persecution from a range of stakeholders because of their work. They may also raise issues directly with ADB about those human rights defenders who could face persecution because of raising concerns about ADB-financed operations.

Advocacy groups, particularly those with a mandate in monitoring public expenditure, transparency, and anticorruption, may monitor ADB-financed projects for accountability, efficiency, and transparency purposes. Advocacy organizations may have valuable information about project or policy implementation that is otherwise unavailable to ADB, which should be considered. When such information relates to concerns, ADB should proactively follow up such information to understand and address the issues, as appropriate.

When responding to such queries from CSOs, staff should consider the following:

Respond to requests for meetings promptly. Each regional department, resident mission, and regional office has a CSO anchor who should be involved in the meeting and who may be able to help provide more information about the advocacy organization.

Prepare for the consultation thoroughly. Staff should research the CSO and the issue about which they want to meet, prepare an agenda, develop ground rules, and share these with all participants in advance. Be familiar with the consultations that have already taken place as part of the project. Organize for interpretation and translation of materials, if required. Allow adequate time for the meeting, recognizing that some CSO representatives may not understand ADB processes and may need extra time for explanations.

Conduct the meeting sensitively. The guidelines in section 3, Principles for Effective Consultation with CSOs, are of particular importance when meeting advocacy organizations. In addition, allow the CSO in question to voice issues of concern, even though these matters might not be priorities for, or even seem directly relevant to, ADB. Be sensitive to cultural differences and address CSOs in plain language, being careful to avoid technical terms, acronyms, professional jargon, or other specialized vocabulary. Be particularly sensitive to gender, age, ethnicity, and religious backgrounds of the participants—conduct the meeting in a way so that all can participate and feel included.

Listen. Discussions with CSOs are an opportunity for staff members to listen, learn, and be influenced as well as to inform and explain. CSOs that act as advocates for vulnerable groups may feel at particular political risk in meeting ADB. Avoid impressions of overconfidence or of being defensive. Take the time to answer questions fully, plainly, and patiently, while also being realistic about what changes can be made.

Follow up. If an answer cannot be provided to a query during the meeting, commit to getting back to the CSO and ensure that an answer is provided within a reasonable time. Prepare a short note to file, including who participated, what was discussed, the major complaints or proposals voiced, general impressions of the encounter, and actions agreed on during the meeting. Include details in back-to-office reports if meetings occurred in the field. Share the meeting notes with the ADB offices concerned with the subjects discussed and the organizations met. Send a follow-up note of thanks for the CSOs' input, acknowledging the major points made or the issues articulated, informing them of any steps that have been (or will be) taken in response to their concerns, and inviting their further comment. Providing feedback is important. Recognize that at times CSOs may not be satisfied with the engagement process or the dialogue. If CSOs perceive that their input is not taken seriously and has no impact, then they may escalate the target of their concerns, for instance, by raising their concerns with the ADB Management or Board, the media, or in public forums.

Advocacy organizations may lead protests outside of ADB's headquarters or field offices (even while the same organization may be participating inside an ADB venue) to draw media attention or create a media moment to be captured. Realize that this is their media strategy and continue to engage with the group through listening and keeping an open mind to ideas or recommendations. In such cases, act respectfully and courteously. Be aware of the safety of protestors. Ask to speak to organizers and hear the issues the protestors want to bring to ADB's attention, receive any documents they may want to share with ADB, and respond to their demands when they are reasonable requests. Examples include requests to meet staff to bring issues to their attention and requests to provide feedback to their concerns. Note that from time to time, such protests are in the format of online advocacy campaigns. Likewise, stay engaged as much as reasonable, and note the issues and concerns the participants are raising. ADB should monitor concerns systematically and ensure each concern is appropriately responded to.

Reputational issues may arise when advocacy organizations use media or social media to articulate their issues. Staff may seek DOC's support in risk assessment, positioning, and media monitoring. Staff may seek the NGOC's advice and support, as needed, to address queries from advocacy organizations.

Frequently Asked Questions

Q **How do I identify reliable CSOs in the sector where I am implementing my project?**
Many resident missions maintain lists of CSOs with which ADB regularly interacts. The ADB and Civil Society webpage features links to the Civil Society Briefs, which feature CSO directories and umbrella organizations. Other sites also list CSO networks, including the list of NGO Databases and Directories.[132] See section 4 for further information on identifying CSOs.

Q **What is ADB's accreditation process for CSOs?**
ADB does not maintain an accreditation system for CSOs, except for the specific purpose of attendance at the ADB annual meeting. For CSO accreditation at the annual meeting, review the process which is laid out in the annual Board report on the attendance of CSOs at the annual meeting (see for example, the 2020 report on the process for the 2021 ADB Annual Meeting).[133] When ADB engages CSOs as consultants, ADB's Guidelines on the Use of Consultants apply.

Q **Do projects do better with or without CSOs?**
An Independent Evaluation Department analysis of rated projects implemented during 2000–2004 compared similar sector projects implemented with CSO engagement with those implemented in the absence of CSO engagement and showed that projects with CSO engagement were more likely to be rated as successful. Country assistance program evaluations for Nepal and the Philippines have concluded that beneficiary participation, including that channeled through CSOs, seems to improve project results. CSOs have also played a crucial role in resolving complaints to the Office of the Special Project Facilitator, showing how CSOs can take a facilitative role. Roles may depend on the situation and need to be agreed upon early and monitored. CSOs can act as useful observers, channels of communication, and intermediaries between complainants, in bridging cultural gaps, as advisors to complainants, or as representatives of affected people.

Q **How do I respond to CSO requests for information?**
The AIP establishes the requirements for information disclosure. Many documents of interest to CSOs are available on ADB website pages and provide guidance on responding to CSO information requests. See section 5, Engaging with Advocacy Organizations, for further information on how to respond to requests from CSOs.

Q **How do I organize a consultation with CSOs?**
Consultations with CSOs, as well as those conducted with other stakeholders, require proper preparation. See section 3 for further advice.

Q **How do I respond to critical CSOs?**
ADB has considerable experience in communicating with CSOs that criticize or oppose ADB-financed activities for one reason or another. Engagement with watchdog CSOs has often revealed shortcomings in projects and has helped resolve or prevent problems. Even in cases where CSOs promote a rigid agenda to which ADB cannot completely agree, there is value in maintaining an open dialogue. In only a minority of cases do CSOs totally reject engagement and instead opt for a firmly oppositional stance, typically for ideological or political reasons. See section 5, Engaging with Advocacy Organizations, for further advice.

---

[132] The Global Development Research Center. NGO Databases and Directories.
[133] Footnote 129.

Q **How do I find a reliable CSO to help with my project?**

The NGOC, CSO anchors, resident missions, divisional colleagues, and ADB communities of practice and committees are excellent places to begin looking for potential CSO partners for a project. Bilateral and multilateral donors, as well as CSO apex and umbrella organizations, can also be useful sources of information. ADB's Civil Society Briefs provide an overview of the civil society landscape in several countries.[134] See section 4 for further advice.

Q **With what kind of CSOs does ADB collaborate?**

ADB works mainly, but not exclusively, with developmental CSOs, i.e., organizations that address concerns such as social and humanitarian issues relating to development, individual and community welfare and well-being, and poverty alleviation, as well as environmental and natural resource protection, management, and improvement. Research and academic organizations and institutes may also qualify as CSOs and work with ADB in a range of roles. See section 2 for types of CSOs that ADB engages with.

Q **What kind of funding does ADB offer CSOs?**

ADB does not maintain a dedicated general small grants fund for CSOs as many other development actors do. The JFPR finances small-scale investment projects that directly target poverty reduction and have a link to ADB-financed loan projects. CSOs are often engaged to help implement JFPR-financed projects. See section 2 for further information on JFPR.

Q **How accountable are CSOs?**

CSOs increasingly respond to the challenge of matching the level of accountability demanded by many governments, media, and the public. Most reputable CSOs establish and make publicly known the standards to which they adhere. Many commit to national or international codes of conduct. In a growing number of countries, ratings and accreditation systems are used to assess CSO accountability, capacity, and performance. See section 4 for further information.

Q **What roles can we expect to CSOs for NSO transactions?**

CSO services are typically procured by the client in nonsovereign operations (NSOs). On sensitive projects, CSOs may undertake roles implementing or monitoring safeguards and/or gender action plans. CSOs may also be borrowers or clients in NSOs, particularly when ADB provides financing to financial intermediaries (see Box 8). CSOs may be consulted under NSOs or interviewed as part of extended annual review report missions. Section 5 describes the roles for CSOs in NSOs.

Q **What do I do if particular stakeholders do not want to work with CSOs?**

Explain that it is ADB's policy to cooperate with CSOs and that such cooperation has yielded positive benefits in other countries. Determine if the concern relates only to particular CSOs, or if it extends more broadly. Staff may consider keeping relevant stakeholders informed of meetings with CSOs or inviting stakeholder representatives to participate in discussions with CSOs.

Section 5, Engaging Civil Society Organizations and Respecting Governments, describes how to deal with sensitivities around CSO engagement in ADB-financed operations.

---

[134] ADB. Civil Society Briefs.

6

Responsibilities for Civil Society Organization Engagement Within ADB

Operations Departments

The core of Asian Development Bank's (ADB's) work is carried out through its regional departments and the Private Sector Operations Department. The processing, implementation, and monitoring of projects take place in these departments. Thus, communication and consultation with civil society organizations (CSOs) in ADB-financed activities occur primarily through the operations departments.

Strengthening relationships with stakeholders in developing member countries (DMCs) is the responsibility of ADB's operations departments which serve as the contact points for CSOs directly involved in, or concerned with, projects, programs, country assistance, or regional integration initiatives.

Specific examples of operations department responsibilities include broad consultations with CSOs in project identification and planning activities, technical and project-related consultations and discussions with CSOs, defining roles for CSOs in specific project activities, consultations concerning the country partnership strategy (CPS) relating to the country concerned, compiling information about CSOs relevant to specific activities, and meeting CSO requests for project-related information.

Resident Missions

As ADB's principal representative in the field, a standard function of every resident mission is managing CSO relations in the country where the resident mission is located. In addition, ADB's Resident Mission Policy recognizes the creation of solid partnerships with CSOs and other development stakeholders as a key partnership objective.

Most resident missions have appointed a staff member to serve as CSO anchor or focal point, usually in conjunction with either social development or external relations responsibilities. The role of this staff member typically includes addressing CSO queries, facilitating contact with project staff, organizing briefings and consultations, providing input into ADB's annual report on cooperation with CSOs, maintaining a database of CSO contacts, and keeping ADB headquarters staff informed of developments in the country's CSO sector.

See the ADB and Civil Society webpage for more information on the ADB resident mission CSO anchors.

BOX 27

In late 2019, ADB's Mongolia Resident Mission established a CAC to facilitate CSO engagement in country programming and the development of ADB and Mongolia's CPS for 2021–2024. The CAC originally comprised seven members representing major CSO networks and alliances, operating in sectors that are relevant to ADB operations in Mongolia. The CAC serves as a key mechanism to share information with CSOs, organize consultation processes on specific projects, utilize capacity building products, and ensure that CSO views are represented during CPS development.

ADB = Asian Development Bank, CAC = Civil Society Advisory Committee, CPS = country partnership strategy, CSO = civil society organization.
Source: Asian Development Bank.

Sustainable Development and Climate Change Department

Among other roles, the Sustainable Development and Climate Change Department (SDCC) serves as an anchor for sector-based and thematic strategic directions in key areas of ADB operations, including climate change and disaster risk management, education, energy, environment, gender, fragile and conflict-affected situations (FCAS), governance, health, poverty alleviation, and transport. SDCC's divisions and units regularly engage CSOs to inform them of their work in these areas. This includes information relating to assessments, events, reports, special initiatives, and technical assistance (TA) projects.

See ADB's Focus Areas webpage for more information.

NGO and Civil Society Center and the Civil Society Network

ADB created the NGO and Civil Society Center (NGOC) in 2001 to strengthen cooperation with CSOs and to respond to their concerns. Located within SDCC, the NGOC holds the primary institutional responsibility for developing, implementing, and assessing general policy and practice relating to cooperation with CSOs. The NGOC provides advice, contacts, and information to ADB departments and offices relating to CSO engagement. The NGOC is also ADB's general focal point for liaison with CSOs, and likewise serves as a knowledge resource center for ADB's interaction with CSOs. The NGOC does not serve as a "gatekeeper" or "screen" for CSO contact with ADB. However, it can facilitate connections between CSOs and relevant staff members in cases in which direct relations between the two have not yet been established. It also provides background briefings for staff members meeting with CSO representatives. In cases in which CSOs wish to meet staff members from several departments or offices at about the same time, the NGOC typically assists with such meetings.

The NGOC is responsible for (i) developing ADB guidelines and providing advice on consultation involving CSOs and other stakeholders; (ii) elaborating, implementing, and reporting on ADB's overall program of communications and collaboration with CSOs, and managing ADB's policy on cooperation with CSOs; (iii) implementing selected TA projects supporting the role of CSOs in development; (iv) providing training on consultative and participatory practices and on working with CSOs to develop staff and institutional capacity; and (v) maintaining a centralized information database relating to CSOs.

The NGOC is responsible for organizing the civil society program under ADB's annual meeting, and for accreditation of the CSO accreditation program for the annual meeting (see section 5 for more information).

The NGOC also coordinates the network of CSO anchors in resident missions, representative offices, and ADB headquarters. The network shares experience, insights, information, and knowledge relating to ADB's interaction with CSOs. Part of the information shared is ADB's Civil Society Briefs. These briefs contain information on CSOs in a DMC, including the capacity and focus of civil society, a list of some of the larger, well-established CSOs, and the enabling environment and requirements for legal registration for CSOs.

The NGOC can assist resident missions with the CSO engagement aspects of CPS preparation, including
- (i)   preparation of the CSO component of the stakeholder analysis;
- (ii)   facilitation of the country team's preparation of a CPS participation plan in line with ADB's business processes, e.g., NGOC can help identify key CSOs and provide advice on how to engage with these organizations;
- (iii)   preparation of a communications plan to ensure information on the timeline and opportunities to comment online and at meetings reach CSOs;
- (iv)   preparation of a CPS supplementary background document on civil society space;
- (v)   preparation and facilitation of consultations with CSOs, incorporating good practice for consultations;
- (vi)   conducting a desk review of relevant CSO literature and data;
- (vii)   gathering evidence that CSO inputs were duly considered by ADB;
- (viii)   arranging a peer reviewer from a CSO; and
- (ix)   documenting the CSO engagement process.

See the ADB and Civil Society webpage for more information on the NGOC, including the CSO anchors.

Department of Communications

The Department of Communications (DOC) is responsible for preparing news releases relating to CSO-related issues. Teams may consult with DOC on possible news releases on projects with a major CSO component, and workshops and conferences featuring CSO participation of note. DOC also maintains ADB's website, including the web pages relating to civil society, and publishes briefs, handbooks, and other materials on CSO-related topics. DOC can recommend ways in which CSOs can be used to disseminate information concerning ADB-financed activities. This includes umbrella and apex CSOs as well as nongovernment research institutions.

See ADB's Media Contacts webpage for more information on DOC.

Office of Anticorruption and Integrity

The Office of Anticorruption and Integrity is the ADB office responsible for ensuring strengthening governance, integrity, and transparency in ADB-financed, ADB-assisted, and ADB-supported activity relating to corrupt, fraudulent, coercive, or collusive practices, abuse, conflict of interest, obstructive practices, and violations of ADB sanctions. It investigates specific integrity violations, including from CSOs, and promotes integrity among ADB's stakeholders, including among CSOs.

See the Anticorruption and Integrity webpage for more information on OAI.

Representative Offices

Representative offices in Europe, Japan, and North America play a critical role in building and maintaining ADB's profile, given their proximity to key stakeholders, their operational and economic expertise, and their understanding of the unique cultural and communications aspects of the country or region in which they are based. These three offices are key ADB communicators that work to expand and strengthen ADB's interactions with the media, opinion leaders, and decision-makers in the country or region concerned. These include influential CSOs located in the geographic regions for which the representative offices are responsible.

See ADB's Where We Work webpage for more information on representative offices and resident missions.

Accountability Mechanism

ADB's Accountability Mechanism offers people adversely affected by ADB-financed projects an opportunity to voice concerns and seek solutions to their problems, and likewise to report alleged violations of ADB's operational policies and procedures. The mechanism comprises two separate, but related functions: the consultation phase and the compliance review phase.

The consultation phase assists people adversely affected by ADB-financed projects to find solutions to their problems. It is led by ADB's special project facilitator. The compliance phase establishes ADB's accountability in its operations by providing a forum in which project-affected people (and in special circumstances, any ADB Board member) can file requests for compliance review.

The Compliance Review Panel is responsible for this phase. Most complaints that reach the accountability mechanism have been prepared by, or with the support of, CSOs. In recognition of this fact, staff of the accountability mechanism regularly meet with CSO representatives in Manila and carry out an active outreach program that engages local, national, and international CSOs in many countries.

See the Accountability Mechanism webpage for more information.

Appendixes

APPENDIX 1

Strategy 2030 Operational Priorities and Potential Roles for Civil Society Organizations

Addressing remaining poverty and reducing inequalities

What does the Operational Plan for Priority (OPP) 1 say?

Enhancing civil society engagement to promote participation and social inclusion, and to reduce inequalities. Asian Development Bank (ADB) will continue to work with developing member countries (DMCs) to identify opportunities for greater civil society engagement in project design and implementation. Provisions within policy loans and other financial instruments will bring governments closer to citizens by incentivizing the meaningful use of citizen-oriented design, feedback, and accountability mechanisms, especially using new digital technologies. Where possible, projects will be linked to DMCs' Open Government Partnership commitments to promote collaborative approaches with other multilateral actors. Enhancing partnerships with relevant institutions, including civil society organizations (CSOs), to generate knowledge, share good practices, and improve policy dialogue.[1]

How can CSOs contribute?

Policy and strategy review and formulation:
  (i)   Facilitate the participation of poor, vulnerable, and excluded groups and communities in consultations on policies and strategies.
  (ii) Contribute to consultations by representing the diverse views and perspectives of the poor, vulnerable, and excluded.

Programs and projects:
  (i)   Contribute to program and project design by making sure it is responsive to the needs and concerns of the poor, vulnerable, and excluded; and specific groups such as women and youth.
  (ii) Ensure that information about programs and projects reaches the poor, vulnerable, and excluded persons and groups in remote communities through consultations, house-to-house visits, using local languages, and the use of mass and social media.
  (iii) Develop the capacities of poor, vulnerable, and excluded persons, groups, and communities in poverty reduction and participatory governance endeavors (e.g., developing and expanding businesses, marketing, appropriate technology, information technology, primary health care, climate and disaster resilience, management, gender and development, and others).
  (iv) Implement programs and projects related to the seven operational priority areas in poor and disadvantaged communities.
  (v)   Participate in multistakeholder monitoring and evaluation of programs and projects to ensure compliance with environmental and social safeguard policies and plans.

---

[1]   ADB. 2019. *Strategy 2030 Operational Plan for Priority 1: Addressing Remaining Poverty and Reducing Inequalities, 2019-2024.* Manila.

(vi)   Conduct or participate in impact evaluations, including baseline surveys and uptake of lessons from programs and projects targeting the poor, vulnerable, and excluded.

(vii)   Develop knowledge products for poor, vulnerable, and excluded groups and communities.

(viii) Assist ADB and governments to promote project-specific grievance redress mechanisms and access to ADB's Accountability Mechanism.

Roles and tasks that can be done by people's organizations and community-based organizations:

(i)   Ensure that programs and projects intended to benefit their members and interests are responsive to the conditions in their communities, including when there is a change in circumstances in the communities (such as in the case of disaster or conflict).

(ii)   Ensure that all members of their communities, regardless of gender, age, disability, sexual orientation, gender identity, religion, ethnicity, or political affiliation are informed and given the opportunity to meaningfully participate equally and benefit from ADB programs and projects.

(iii)   Actively participate in programs and projects to make sure benefits come to them and other members of their communities and sectors.

Accelerating progress in gender equality

What does the OPP2 say?

At the country operational level, ADB capacity should be built to better manage multistakeholder partnerships, particularly with the prospects of having to address more complex gender equality issues such as women's climate change resilience and gender-based violence, involving multiple government agencies, CSOs, private sector enterprises, foundations, and partners. It will also strengthen gender-related capacity development of civil society partners involved in ADB operations. ADB will expand innovation and knowledge solutions on gender by expanding knowledge partnerships externally with think tanks, universities, foundations, CSOs, and bilateral and multilateral partners while internally between operations departments and knowledge departments; regularly engaging DMCs, such as line ministries, gender focal agencies, private sector and civil society partners, and in-country think tanks in prioritizing and generating ADB gender knowledge work to enhance client knowledge relevance.[2]

How can CSOs contribute?

Policy and strategy review and formulation:

(i)   Conduct gender analyses and assessments.

(ii)   Participate in the formulation of gender equality and women's empowerment (GEWE)-related policies and strategies.

(iii)   Demonstrate and implement GEWE-related strategies and actions.

(iv)   Disseminate GEWE-related policies and strategies.

(v)   Participate in the formulation of sector road maps such as on climate change resilience, urban development, rural development and food security, and governance, to bring in GEWE perspectives.

(vi)   Participate in the formulation of midterm review instruments to ensure inclusion of GEWE dimensions.

(vii)   Conduct gender audits as contribution to midterm reviews of country programs.

---

[2]   ADB. 2019. *Strategy 2030 Operational Plan for Priority 2: Accelerating Progress In Gender Equality, 2019–2024.* Manila.

Programs and projects:
  (i)   At project identification and design, gather and analyze sex-disaggregated data and information with emphasis on participation of women and girls in development, gender issues and gender gaps that might support or prevent women and girls from benefiting from project results and other country context inequality issues, including gender-based violence and harmful sociocultural and gender norms.
  (ii)   Participate in the formulation of project gender designs and gender action plans (GAPs).
  (iii)   Participate in the implementation of GAPs.
  (iv)   Conduct monitoring and evaluation of GAPs.
  (v)   Participate in the crafting of GEWE-related knowledge products resulting from project implementation.
  (vi)   CSOs, such as women's organizations, are also potential partners in small-scale civil works to support women's employment during construction and/or operations and maintenance works.

Note: CSOs with expertise or experience in gender equality and women's empowerment should be actively and effectively involved in projects classified as Category I: gender equity theme (GEN) and Category II: effective gender mainstreaming (EGM), wherever this is feasible.

Roles and tasks that people's organizations and community-based organizations:
  (i)   Ensure the participation of marginalized and vulnerable women and girls in community consultations and meetings.
  (ii)   Disseminate information to women and girls who are affected by projects and programs.
  (iii)   Monitor civil works contracts in the context of preventing sexual exploitation and abuse of local populations.

Tackling climate change, building climate and disaster resilience, and enhancing environmental sustainability

What does the OPP3 say?

Build partnerships with think tanks, nongovernment organizations (NGOs), academe, and private sector. Partnerships with the United Nations agencies on the environment and with international and regional networks, institutions, and NGOs will be leveraged to tap into the expertise, resources, and networks of these organizations.[3]

How can CSOs contribute?

Policy and strategy review and formulation:
  (i)   At pre-country partnership strategy (CPS) formulation, participate in assessments, including the design of assessments, and conduct analyses on the differentiated impacts of climate change and disaster risk across vulnerable sectors.
  (ii)   Participate in the formulation, dissemination, and implementation of climate change and disaster risk management national policies and sustainable development strategies.
  (iii)   Participate in the formulation of monitoring and evaluation instruments.
  (iv)   Conduct or participate in impact evaluations.

---

[3]   ADB. 2019. *Strategy 2030 Operational Plan for Priority 3: Tackling Climate Change, Building Climate and Disaster Resilience, and Enhancing Environmental Sustainability, 2019–2024.* Manila.

Programs and projects:

(i)   During project identification and design, gather climate change, disaster risk information and data, and conduct analyses on the differentiated impacts on project-affected people (PAP).

(ii) Participate in the formulation of the safeguards and social dimensions of the project administration manual (PAM), GAP, report and recommendation of the President (RRP), and in the crafting of design and monitoring framework (DMF) indicators on climate and disaster resilience.

(iii) Implement climate change and disaster risk management programs and projects.

(iv) Conduct monitoring and evaluation of safeguards and social dimensions of the PAM, RRP, and DMF indicators on climate change and disaster risk management.

Note: CSOs with expertise or experience in climate change and/or disaster risk management may have capacities to perform multihazard risk assessments and review or enhance local disaster risk reduction plans, policies, and strategies. They can also provide technical assistance (TA) to local authorities in response, recovery, and preparedness for pandemics and other disasters triggered by natural hazards.

Roles and tasks that people's organizations and community-based organizations:

(i)   Ensure the participation of marginalized and vulnerable in community consultations and meetings, including women and youth.

(ii) Improving access to green finance for small entrepreneurs and women-led businesses.

(iii) Raising awareness of the wider population and youth about the consequences of climate change.

(iv) Improving the population's access to climate information.

(v)   Assist local authorities in disaster response and rescues, including management of evacuation centers and internally displaced persons.

Making cities more livable

What do Strategy 2030 and the OPP4 say?

ADB will consider the various needs of all those living, working, and studying in cities through participatory processes involving businesses, academia, and CSOs.[4] ADB will engage with citizens and CSOs throughout various phases of the project cycle. ADB considers engagement with CSOs vital to its operations because they provide a platform where voices of the most vulnerable can be heard, creating stronger links, and facilitating beneficiaries' participation in ADB operations. They also provide ADB with valuable knowledge and expertise and a testing ground for innovative approaches that can be piloted. Facilitate the enhancement of citizen-centric approaches and effective partnerships among the government, private sector, and CSOs to improve service provision aimed at making cities more livable and inclusive.[5]

---

[4]   ADB. 2018. *Strategy 2030: Achieving a Prosperous, Inclusive, Resilient, and Sustainable Asia and the Pacific.* Manila. para. 56.

[5]   ADB. 2019. *Strategy 2030 Operational Plan for Priority 4: Making Cities More Livable, 2019–2024.* Manila.

How can CSOs contribute?

Policy and strategy review and formulation:

(i)   Conduct assessments on urban health, urban mobility, gender equality and social inclusion, environmental sustainability, climate change and disaster risk management, heritage conservation; and analyses urbanization impact to the vulnerable and marginalized populations.

(ii) Gather citizens' inputs and assist in formulating "state of cities" reports, including validating data and reports.

(iii) Assist in the formulation of urban development strategies to improve delivery of services to marginalized sectors such as social protection, social safeguards, and consumer protection.

(iv) Work with cities in designing and formulating citizen-centric and inclusion frameworks for vulnerable populations in urban settings such as children, persons with disabilities, older persons, and migrants.

(v)   Raise citizens' and governments' awareness on urban development issues and information on accessing services especially among migrants and the homeless, and how or whether these groups are accessing services.

(vi) Monitor and conduct evaluation of urban development plans and strategies.

Programs and projects:

(i)   At project identification and design, conduct assessments on urban health, urban mobility, gender equality and social inclusion, environmental sustainability, heritage, climate change and disaster risk management, and analyses on the impacts to PAPs.

(ii) Participate in the formulation of the safeguards and social dimensions of the PAM, GAP, RRP; and in the crafting of DMF indicators on livable cities.

(iii) Identify, design; and implement programs and projects on urban health, urban mobility, gender equality and social inclusion, environmental sustainability, heritage, climate change; and disaster risk management.

(iv) Ensure the participation of people's organizations and community-based organizations such as homeowners' associations, housing cooperatives; consumer and user groups for water, sanitation, and electricity; and transport groups, in project design and implementation.

(v)   Conduct monitoring and evaluation of safeguards and social dimensions of the PAM, RRP. and DMF indicators on livable cities.

(vi) Maintenance and operations of facilities.

Roles and tasks that can be done by people's organizations and community-based organizations:

(i)   Ensure the participation of marginalized and vulnerable in community consultations and meetings especially those that belong to home-owners' associations; women's organizations; groups representing urban youth; housing coops; consumer groups for water, sanitation, and electricity; and transport groups.

(ii) Build cohesion between the grassroots-level needs and government-level policies.

(iii) Lobby for local legislation that may pertain to tariff rates, consumer rights, and representation in local boards and committees.

Promoting rural development and food security

What does the OPP5 say?

Implementation of rural development programs will require an enabling environment, capable local governments and decentralized supervision, fiscal and nonfiscal incentives to attract and retain investors, and collaboration of CSOs and consumer protection and social safeguards groups to watch over social protection. This will require investments in local government capacity building and support for nongovernment and CSOs. ADB will strengthen partnerships in finance, implementation, monitoring and evaluation, and policy and knowledge solutions. These will range from upstream partnerships with development and research communities in view of the international and policy context, academia, and applied research institutions, to downstream project partnerships with cofinanciers and local entities, including CSOs.[6]

How can CSOs contribute?

Policy and strategy review and formulation:
- (i) Conduct assessments, including data collection and analysis, on market connectivity and agricultural value chains, access to finance, agricultural practices, food safety, conditions of rural roads, rural water supply and sanitation, market infrastructure and agrilogistics centers, and analyses on the impacts of vulnerable and marginalized sectors such as poor rural women, boys and girls, persons with disabilities, older persons, and the unemployed.
- (ii) Participate in the formulation and review of policies, strategies, and country programs on rural development and food security.
- (iii) Disseminate information and raise awareness regarding policies and strategies on rural development and food security.
- (iv) Conduct monitoring, evaluation and reviews of country programs on rural development and food security to ensure positive impact on the lives of the marginalized and vulnerable sectors.

Programs and projects:
- (i) Conduct assessments on market connectivity and agricultural value chains, agricultural practices, food safety, conditions of rural roads, market infrastructure and agrilogistics centers, and analyses on the impacts to PAPs and their environments.
- (ii) Participate in the formulation of the stakeholders' communication strategy, safeguards. and social dimensions of the PAM, GAP, RRP; and in the crafting of DMF indicators on rural development and food security.
- (iii) Identify, design, and implement programs and projects on rural development and food security.
- (iv) Organize rural community-based organizations such as women farmers' cooperatives youth for food security groups, and environmental groups, in rural, urban, and coastal settings, toward sustainability of programs and projects by building on existing promising initiatives and guided by good practice.
- (v) Conduct monitoring and evaluation of safeguards and social dimensions of the PAM, RRP, and DMF indicators for rural development and food security.
- (vi) Provide TA in the maintenance and operations of facilities for food security to people's organizations on the ground.

---

[6] ADB. 2019. *Strategy 2030 Operational Plan for Priority 5: Promoting Rural Development and Food Security, 2019–2024*. Manila.

Note: Some CSOs may have expertise or experience in advanced technologies on irrigation efficiency, sustainable use of land and water resources, climate-smart agricultural practices and improving natural resource management standards, quality control laboratories, halal food certification, and use of information and communication technology to improve food traceability and tracking.

Roles and tasks that can be done by people's organizations and community-based organizations:
- (i) Ensure the participation of marginalized and vulnerable in community consultations and meetings especially those that belong to farmers' cooperatives, fishers' groups, women farmers' cooperatives, youth for food security groups, and environmental groups.
- (ii) Maintain and operate food security facilities such as solar driers, food processing centers, storage facilities, technology and skills centers, small-scale economic hubs, and community markets.
- (iii) Maintain and operate community-owned farming and fishing equipment, including transportation, fishing boats, irrigation systems, and water and sanitation facilities.

Strengthening governance and institutional capacity

What does the OPP6 say?

Strengthening collaboration with CSOs. ADB will work in partnership with a broad range of CSOs to strengthen social accountability and contribute to responsive service delivery in DMCs. Experience shows that civil society engagement improves the quality of ADB operations and contributes to increasing inclusiveness by placing citizens—particularly the poor and marginalized—at the center of the development process. Therefore, ADB will support the maintenance of civil society space in DMCs and the strengthening of the rule of law. ADB will use its convening power to facilitate multistakeholder engagement and leverage the supply and demand sides of governance. For example, ADB engagement with the Open Government Partnership provides a means to support constructive engagement between governments and citizens. ADB will explore opportunities for increasing citizen involvement in designing, implementing, and monitoring ADB operations, including streamlining grants and partnership mechanisms. To better align with the 2030 strategic framework, ADB will undertake a gap analysis to identify priority areas for working with CSOs and develop operational processes and staff instructions to support deeper civil society engagement. Key drivers of transformative change will include promoting digital technology advancement into service delivery in close collaboration with civil society and with a focus on citizen-centric improvements.[7]

How can CSOs contribute?

Policy and strategy review and formulation:
- (i) Conduct policy analyses on governance and diagnostics on national programs for building institutional capacities of government agencies and local authorities.
- (ii) Examine country level practices in engaging CSOs and citizen networks for accountability, transparency, and inclusivity.
- (iii) Participate in the formulation and monitoring of policies, strategies, and country programs on strengthening governance and institutional capacities.

---

[7] ADB. 2019. *Strategy 2030 Operational Plan for Priority 6: Strengthening Governance and Institutional Capacity, 2019–2024.* Manila.

(iv)   Disseminate data and information on fiscal management, budget allocations, and expenditures.

(v)   Implement programs and projects on civic participation and citizenship (e.g., citizens' monitoring, voters' education, legislative lobbying).

CSO participation in ADB's governance and project cycle:

(i)   At project identification and design stage, conduct local governance diagnostics of fiscal or budget data contextualized within ADB's priorities.

(ii)   Examine the capacities of local authorities in terms of (a) access to information; (b) functional capacities—planning, budgeting, and funding execution, community or sector engagement, and program implementation, service delivery; and (c) monitoring and examine local perspective on quality-of-service delivery and priority needs.

(iii)   Participate in the formulation of the safeguards and social dimensions of the PAM, GAP, RRP, and in the crafting of DMF indicators on governance.

(iv)   Implement programs and projects on strengthening governance, accountability, and institutional capacity.

(v)   Conduct monitoring and evaluation of safeguards and social dimensions of the PAM, RRP, and DMF indicators on governance.

(vi)   Crowd-source innovations from citizen groups, including youth groups, to boost demand-side governance, including through use of technology.

Roles and tasks that can be done by people's organizations and community-based organizations:

(i)   Organize and facilitate citizens' monitoring groups, including youth groups, local women's groups, other vulnerable populations, and people's movements.

(ii)   Implement citizens' monitoring activities as part of anticorruption measures in all projects and programs.

Fostering regional cooperation and integration

How can CSOs contribute?

Policy and strategy review and formulation:

(i)   Networks and alliances of CSOs, which are often regionwide, can channel the voice of a range of CSOs across the relevant region on relevant policy and strategies.

(ii)   While consulting all citizens of a country is clearly not feasible, intermediary organizations such as CSOs can help ensure that the views of a broad range of citizens, including those who may be negatively affected by reforms, are heard and considered. CSOs can play an important role in four major areas: facilitation, mobilizing labor, oversight and advocacy, and impact monitoring and evaluation.

(iii)   Mobilization of international CSOs to participate in dialogues among DMCs, particularly in subregional economic cooperation programs such as the Central Asia Regional Economic Cooperation, Greater Mekong Subregion, and South Asia Subregional Economic Cooperation.

CSO participation in fostering regional cooperation and integration programs and projects:
Ensure the voices of border communities are heard in the design and implementation of projects, particularly in relation to issues that cross borders, including health, education, sport, culture, tourism, food safety, agriculture, disasters triggered by natural hazard, emergencies, transport, and trade.

Roles and tasks that can be done by people's organizations and community-based organizations:

(i)   Ensure the protection of rights of migrants, migrant workers, internally displaced persons, including women, older persons and young people, smallholder farmers, population in border areas that may result from development programs, and projects involving two or more countries or those having impacts across borders.

(ii)   Mobilize community responses to cross-border disasters and emergencies, including floods, earthquake, and pest and disease control.

External Resources

Other Multilateral Development Bank Resources on Civil Society Organization Engagement

African Development Bank: https://www.afdb.org/en/topics-and-sectors/topics/civil-society.

European Bank for Reconstruction and Development: https://www.ebrd.com/who-we-are/civil-society-overview.html.

Global Partnership for Social Development (World Bank): https://www.thegpsa.org/.

Inter-American Development Bank: https://www.iadb.org/en/civil-society/home.

Islamic Development Bank Group: https://www.isdb.org/sites/default/files/media/documents/2020-02/IsDB_CSO%20Policy.pdf.

World Bank Group: https://www.worldbank.org/en/about/partners/civil-society.

Development Partners and Civil Society Organization Engagement during the Pandemic

European Union. 2021. *The response of civil society organizations to face the COVID-19 pandemic and the consequent restrictive measures adopted in Europe.* https://www.eesc.europa.eu/sites/default/files/files/qe-02-21-011-en-n.pdf.

OECD. 2020. *Digital Transformation and the Futures of Civic Space to 2030.* Development Policy Paper. Paris: OECD Publishing. https://www.oecd.org/publications/digital-transformation-and-the-futures-of-civic-space-to-2030-79b34d37-en.htm.

UNHCR. 2020. https://www.unhcr.org/en-au/2020-ngo-consultations-on-the-covid-19-response.html.

UNICEF. 2020. https://www.unicef.org/media/67516/file/Partnership-Management-Between-UNICEF-and-Civil-Society-Organizations.pdf.

Civil Society Organization Assessment Tools

SIDA. 2002. The Octagon. A tool for the assessment of strengths and weaknesses in NGOs. Stockholm. https://resourcecentre.savethechildren.net/node/10076/pdf/the-octagon_1742.pdf.

UNDP. 2010. *A Users Guide to Civil Society Assessments.* UNDP. New York.

USAID. Civil Society Assessment Tool. USAID. Washington, DC. https://pdf.usaid.gov/pdf_docs/PA00XD1Q.pdf.

USAID with ICNL, FHI360. 2020. 2019 Civil Society Organization Sustainability Index – For Asia. Washington, DC. https://www.fhi360.org/sites/default/files/media/documents/csosi-asia-2019-report.pdf.

Civil Society Organization Self-Assessment and Strengthening Toolkits

CIVICUS. 2014. *Accountability for Civil Society by Civil Society: A Guide to Self-Regulation Initiatives.* CIVICUS. Johannesburg. https://www.civicus.org/images/stories/CIVICUS%20Self-regulation%20Guide%20Eng%202014.pdf.

Commonwealth Foundation. 2009. *Civil Society Accountability: Principles and Practice. A toolkit for civil society organisations in the Pacific region.* London. http://commonwealthfoundation.com/wp-content/uploads/2012/12/Civil_society_accountability_toolkit_Pacific.pdf.

European Union. 2012. *Mappings and Civil Society Assessments: A Study of past, present and future trends.* European Union. Belgium.

Philippine Council for NGO Certification. Simplified Organizational Self-Assessment Guide for NGOs/Foundations. https://drive.google.com/file/d/1pvf3Lka4JqUhzYET1ywCGPpD8iBIWA_A/view.

Philippine Council for NGO Certification. 2008. *Guidebook on the Basics of NGO Governance.* funded by Japan Social Development Fund and administered by the World Bank. Manila.

UNDP. 2006. *UNDP and Civil Society Organizations: A Toolkit for Strengthening Partnerships.* UNDP. New York. https://sustainabledevelopment.un.org/content/documents/2141UNDP%20and%20Civil%20Society%20Organizations%20a%20Toolkit%20for%20Strengthening%20Partnerships.pdf.

Evaluating Civil Society Investment Programs

European Commission. 2008. *Evaluation of EC aid channelled through civil society organisations.* https://ecdpm.org/publications/evaluation-ec-aid-channelled-civil-society-organisations/.

L. Kelly, R. David, and C. Roche. 2008. *Guidance on M&E for Civil Society Programs: Prepared for AusAID Program Managers.* Government of Australia.

OECD DAC. 2013. Evaluation Insights September 2013. *Support to Civil Society. Emerging Evaluation Lessons.* INTRAC. https://www.oecd.org/dac/evaluation/Evaluation%20Insight%20Civil%20Society%20FINAL%20for%20print%20and%20WEB%2020131004.pdf.

Engaging Civil Society Organizations in Sectors and Themes–Additional Resources

Gender Equality and Social Inclusion

ADB. 2019. *Mongolia: Moving Gender Equality Forward through Civil Society Engagement.* https://www.adb.org/sites/default/files/project-documents/52314/52314-001-tar-en.pdf.

European Union. *Civil society as an advocate for the rights of persons with disabilities in government decision-making.* https://www.euneighbours.eu/en/east-south/stay-informed/projects/civil-society-advocate-rights-persons-disabilities-government.

FAO. *Gender and Land Rights Database* (Note: the database includes CSOs doing work on various aspects of gender and land rights at country levels.) http://www.fao.org/gender-landrights-database/country-profiles/en/.

Promundo and UNFPA. 2016. *Strengthening CSO-Government Partnerships to Scale Up Approaches Engaging Men and Boys for Gender Equality and SRHR: A Tool for Action.* Washington, DC: Promundo-US and New York City, NY: UNFPA. https://www.unfpa.org/sites/default/files/pub-pdf/50694_-_Scaling_up_Men_and_Boys_-_revised.pdf.

Red Cross. *Taking Action on Social Inclusion of Older People (TASIOP)* https://redcross.eu/projects/taking-action-for-and-with-older-people-in-society.

Food and Agriculture

FAO. 2013. *FAO Strategy for Partnerships with Civil Society Organizations.* https://sustainabledevelopment.un.org/content/documents/2213fao%20strategies%20csos.pdf.

Health

V. Bhargava. 2021. *Engaging Civil Society Organizations to Enhance the Effectiveness of COVID-19 Response Programs in Asia and the Pacific.* ADB The Governance Brief Issue 42 2021. Asian Development Bank, Manila, Philippines. https://www.adb.org/sites/default/files/publication/689831/governance-brief-042-civil-society-covid-19-asia-pacific.pdf.

S.L. Greer et al. 2017. *Civil Society and Health.* World Health Organization. https://books.google.com.ph/books?id=xXeyDwAAQBAJ&source=gbs_navlinks_s.

J. Kanthor et al. 2014. *Engaging Civil Society in Health Finance and Governance: A Guide for Practitioners.* Bethesda, MD: Health Finance & Governance Project, Abt Associates Inc. https://www.hfgproject.org/wp-content/uploads/2015/09/Engaging-Civil-Society-in-Health-Finance-and-Governance_Guide-for-Practitioners.pdf.

USAID. *Combating HIV and AIDS Through Partnerships with Civil Society.* https://www.usaid.gov/global-health/health-areas/hiv-and-aids/technical-areas/combating-hiv-and-aids-through-partnerships.

Water, Sanitation, and Hygiene

C. Fonseca et al. 2020. *Civil society influence in drinking water, sanitation and water resources budgets: four pathways for change.* IRC WASH. https://www.ircwash.org/resources/civil-society-influence-drinking-water-sanitation-and-water-resources-budgets-four.

Transport and Mobility

Civitas Elan. *Citizen Engagement in the Field of Mobility.* European Union. https://civitas.eu/sites/default/files/citizen_engagement_in_the_field_of_mobility_1.pdf.

Governance

Funds for NGOs. *Civil Society Organisations (CSO) Programme: Enhancing CSOs' contribution to governance and development processes in Mongolia.* https://www2.fundsforngos.org/civil-society/civil-society-organisations-cso-programme-enhancing-csos-contribution-governance-development-processes-mongolia/.

Open Government Partnership. *Civil Society Participation to Improve LGU Service Delivery (PH0042).* https://www.opengovpartnership.org/members/philippines/commitments/PH0042/.

APPENDIX 3
Example Framework Agreement Call For Expression of Interest

INVITATION FOR EXPRESSION OF INTEREST (EOI) FOR EMPANELMENT OF FIRMS UNDER A FRAMEWORK AGREEMENT

Deadline for submission of EOI: [INSERT DATE]

The Asian Development Bank (ADB)'s Sustainable Development and Climate Change Department (SDCC) and [relevant department] seeks to empanel 4 to 6 firms under framework agreements to render community engagement assistance to developing member countries (DMCs) with ADB-financed projects in water sector projects and technical assistance in [relevant region]. International civil society organizations (CSOs), or coalitions of CSOs are specifically encouraged to apply.

The framework agreement is being financed by X, Y, and Z project/TA [insert names of projects/TA], which were approved and declared effective by ADB on [insert approval/effectivity dates]. The [grant/loan/TAs] is financed on a grant basis by ADB's [insert fund sources] and is expected to be completed by [end dates]. **OR** An indicative list of projects for which the Framework Agreement will apply is included at Annex 1.

It is intended that the panel will support [relevant region] DMCs' ([list DMCs]) water sector projects in the following two focus areas:

(i) **Community Health Awareness Raising and Behavior Change Programs**: support to one or more DMCs in the development and deployment of a water, sanitation and hygiene (WASH) community health awareness raising and behavior change program which may include: designing a culturally-relevant community health and behavior change awareness campaign, including key messaging for WASH behavior change (e.g., Community Led Total Sanitation [CLTS] and Participatory Hygiene and Sanitation Transformation [PHAST], both demand-driven models of behavior change), WASH in schools, No Open Defecation (NOD) and other WASH campaigns (as appropriate to the DMC); provide the DMC National Health Department [or relevant IA] with expert advice on the optimum delivery methods and channels for the awareness raising and behavior change campaign, including videos, community theatre, non-textual graphical illustrations, radio, public health announcements, as suitable for each DMC; assist in the development and deployment of the community awareness raising and behavior change campaign.

(ii) **Community Engagement on Water Sector Projects**: support to one or more DMCs in community consultation on water sector projects which may include: development and deployment of a community stakeholder engagement plan, working with urban/peri-urban/rural communities and/or informal settlements; facilitate consultation with project-affected people, drawing on the local context, local languages, dialects and idioms, and using participatory approaches that are culturally-sensitive; provide translations of community engagement and outreach materials in local languages; prepare studies and reports for ADB-financed projects in the water sector on issues, including community willingness to pay studies, assessment of user needs and baseline assessments of hygiene awareness and practice, and evaluation of community engagement processes.

Panel firms will have expertise in one or both of the focus areas, with experience in at least one of the DMCs listed.

The empaneled firms will contribute to supporting the DMC(s) in their community engagement in water sector projects. ADB reserves the right to extend the framework for operational reasons or if additional funding becomes available.

The entire selection process involves two distinct stages. Stage 1 involves the empanelment of firms (who may be international CSOs or coalitions of CSOs, or for-profit entities) using the Quality-Based Selection (QBS) method. Under Stage 2, when a need for a service under the framework agreement arises, ADB intends generally to advertise the specific assignment/s to the empaneled firms as call offs. Empaneled firms will be requested to prepare proposals specific to the call offs, which will be evaluated based on Quality- and Cost-Based Selection (QCBS) method, using simplified technical proposals.

Stage 1: Firms will be invited to submit expressions of interest and will be shortlisted based on the firm's management, technical and geographical competence. The EOI should be supported by details of the firm/firms that include name of the firm; country of incorporation; year of incorporation; geographic presence in Asia and the Pacific, including in-country offices and in-country staff, listed by DMC; experience of working in similar areas, including relevant experience in projects/programs of similar nature and complexity in at least one DMC and in at least one of the following two focus areas: (i) community health awareness raising and behavior change; and (ii) community engagement on water sector projects; extent and nature of partnerships/collaborations with local firms/CSOs in each country where the firm has a presence and where the firm is proposing to support the DMC's pandemic emergency response; financial resources, annual turnover (last 5 years), registration details of the firm(s) and details of key personnel. The submitted EOIs will be evaluated by SDCC/[relevant department] based on the above criteria. ADB will issue request for proposals (RfP) to shortlisted firms, requesting them to prepare proposals based around expertise which they have at their disposal and a methodology based on a generic assignment indicated in the detailed terms of reference (TOR). Detailed instructions for submission of proposals will be provided through ADB's consultant management system (CMS) to the shortlisted firms. As a part of the RfP, firms will be required to provide a generic/sample approach and methodology for the aspects of the EOI for which they are applying (which may be one, two or all three of the focus areas) as well as experts available and their fee rates for the various expert bands (including national consultants). Stage 1 will culminate in the signing of framework agreements with each of the empaneled firms. ADB reserves the right to remove firms from the panel for reasons, including poor performance, unwillingness to bid for call offs or widespread lack of availability of experts. ADB also reserves the right to add additional firms to the panel either directly or following a further competitive process.

Under Stage 2, ADB intends to generally advertise the subsequent assignment/s to the empaneled firms as call offs, by inviting the empaneled firms to submit simplified technical proposals for the same. A total of [insert number] call offs are expected over the course of the 3-year framework arrangement. The proposals will be evaluated based on Quality- and Cost- Based Selection (QCBS) method. A typical call off might be expected to require one or both of the following:
   (i)   community health awareness raising and behavior change programs;
   (ii)   community engagement on water sector projects.

Under each call off, firms will be required to propose delivery of the services in partnership with local firms (who may be CSOs), based in the DMC(s) for which they are expressing interest.

For the support in the two focus areas, it is envisaged that there will be call off with value range of [$XXX,000 to $XXX,000] based on complexity of the assignments and specific needs. ADB reserves the right to structure call offs differently based on the specific needs of the individual assignments. Specific TORs will be advertised for each call off. For smaller value assignments (up to $30,000), ADB reserves the right to directly award these to specific empaneled firms, that it feels are best suited for the assignment.

ADB will engage the consultants following ADB's Procurement Policy (2017, as amended from time to time).

Expression of Interest must be submitted online through ADB's CMS no later than 1,700 hours, [insert date]. Offline/hard copy/soft copy submission of EOIs is not allowed. For any clarifications/information regarding the details of the prospective project and this consultant recruitment, you may wish to contact [insert contact name and e-mail].

Annotated Terms of Reference for Civil Society Organization Anchors

JOB DESCRIPTION
CSO Anchor
(of a Resident Mission, Representative Office, or Regional Department)

1. JOB PURPOSE

The CSO anchor serves as the focal point in the resident missions (RM), representative offices (RO), and regional departments (RD) for overall civil society organization (CSO) and nongovernment organization (NGO) relations; the CSO anchor is responsible for the review, analysis, technical input, and support in ensuring the appropriate implementation and monitoring of Asian Development Bank (ADB) policies, guidelines, and mandates related to cooperation with CSOs and other NGOs, focusing on the country or region in which the position will be based or focused. Anchor work is expected to take up 5%–10% of work hours over the year. It will form a part of the incumbent's yearly performance reviews.

2. EXPECTED OUTPUTS

Build Relations with CSOs through Improved Communications
Build, strengthen, and maintain regular lines of communication with CSOs through meetings, outreach activities, and by responding to correspondence. Organize meetings with relevant CSOs and undertake necessary follow-up. Assist in developing partnerships between CSOs and ADB to improve the formulation, implementation, and monitoring of ADB programs and projects. Anchors are expected to spend time reaching out to and meeting with CSOs and networks, to improve their own knowledge and understanding and to expose an increasing number of CSOs to ADB's work. This time should be included in the 5%–10% of work time to be spent on Anchor work.

Manage a CSO Database
Develop and manage a database or register of CSOs (if appropriate, using CSO Link which includes four modules: contact information, operations, complaints, and a library). Include contact and background information about key CSOs in-country. When possible, include information on issues and concerns raised by CSOs on ADB operations and loans, and other activities involving cooperation with CSOs. Monitor and communicate with project teams ensuring key operational data related to CSO participation in operations are up to date (e.g., project information document, CSO Link).

Support NGO and Civil Society Center (NGOC) Outputs
Provide support to the operations of the NGOC and the ADB-wide Civil Society Network. Coordinate with the NGOC at headquarters (HQ) by sharing knowledge and expertise in CSO engagement. This includes contributing to the Civil Society Concern Papers (March every year) and ADB Annual Report of CSO Cooperation (February each year). Routinely share knowledge and experiences with the CSO anchor network and contribute to internal and external ADB publications. Correspond with NGOC on new developments in civil society and contribute to the work of the CSO anchor network and regional NGOC activities.

Provide Operational Support to Increase CSO Participation in ADB Operations
Monitor CSO activities in country. Share with ADB information about civil society's priority issues, geographical coverage, sector presence, expertise, and concerns in country. Undertake a comprehensive review, analysis, and evaluation of all aspects of ADB operations in country related to cooperation with civil society. Based on this research, provide the necessary technical inputs to support effective CSO participation in country. Support and participate in research on civil society-related matters.

Improve Design Methodology and Analysis
Identify and promote appropriate approaches to and processes for CSO participation in ADB operations. Prepare a consultation and participation plan for the Resident Mission and take charge of its implementation. Using time spent meeting with and discussing issues with CSOs locally, monitor in-country CSO activities of relevance to ADB, determine civil society capacity for collaboration, and clarify CSO–government relations.

Provide guidance to the country director, to NGOC staff, relevant regional department staff, mission leaders, and offices on activities related to methodological design and analysis related to CSOs.

Administrative Support
Ensures timely responses to technical requests from other departments and offices. Provides technical support through timely and correct responses to external requests or inquiries related to CSO matters. Facilitates organization and implementation of CSO-related consultations and workshops—develops workshop or conference structures, budgets, agenda, and implementation plans, including supervision of other technical staff in workshop or conference administration.

3. EDUCATION REQUIREMENTS

Bachelor's degree in relevant field; master's degree preferable

4. RELEVANT EXPERIENCE AND OTHER REQUIREMENTS

- At least 5 years of relevant experience, including experience working in or with CSOs.
- Familiarity with the nature and operations of the CSO sector or civil society in general and in ADB's member countries.
- Familiar with ADB policies and business processes related to CSO cooperation, as well as with other relevant ADB policies and processes. Knowledge and skills in social impact analysis, social assessments, and participatory development.
- Strong capability and background in policy operations analysis. Aptitude for analytical and conceptual thinking. Strong communications skills, including ability to originate high-quality written materials.
- Ability to work and communicate effectively with other ADB staff and with CSO representatives.

5. CORE COMPETENCIES

Technical Knowledge and Skills
- Able to help and advise others based on their specialist area of knowledge and skills.
- Uses technical knowledge and skills to complete complex work.
- Uses technical knowledge and skills to improve work systems.

Client Orientation
- Works to meet the needs of clients according to ADB policies and procedures.
- Communicates often with external clients and seeks to understand and anticipate their needs.
- Works with clients to find ways to meet changing needs.

Achieving Results
- Finds ways to reduce time and cost of completing work.
- Monitors work and progress and makes improvements.
- Works with others to overcome problems and find alternative ways to complete work when necessary.

Working Together
- Provides practical support to teams and encouragement for team members.
- Encourages all team members to work together.
- Sets priorities for the team and ensures they are followed through.
- Communicates proactively with internal clients within the country, region, and CSO anchor network.
- Identifies, develops, and fosters external partnerships.

Learning and Knowledge Sharing
- Learns new skills and knowledge and applies them.
- Continuously finds new solutions to problems.
- Leads the team in sharing knowledge and expertise.

Example of a Civil Society Organization Assessment Questionnaire

This prototype questionnaire may be used for assessing potential civil society organizations (CSOs) that can help determine whether a particular CSO is appropriate to work on an Asian Development Bank (ADB)-financed project.

The prototype questionnaire that appears below is a modified version of the United Nations Development Programme (UNDP) Framework for Selection Criteria in Assessing CSO Capacity, which was published in *UNDP and Civil Society Organizations: A Toolkit for Strengthening Partnerships* (2006).

The following version consists of eight categories: (i) legal status, (ii) credibility, (iii) mission and governance, (iv) constituency and support, (v) technical capacity, (vi) managerial capacity, (vii) administrative capacity, and (viii) financial capacity.

Legal Status

Q **Questions**:
- (i)   Is the CSO legally established?
- (ii)   Has it registered with the appropriate authorities?
- (iii) Is it in compliance with relevant legal or regulatory requirements?
- (iv) Who are its officers?

What to look for: (i) registration details at the appropriate government agency and (ii) legal incorporation documents.

Credibility

Q **Questions**:
- (i)   When was the CSO established?
- (ii)   Why was it created?
- (iii) How has the CSO's organization and scope of operations changed over time?
- (iv) Does the CSO subscribe to a particular code of conduct or ethics code?
- (v)   Has it been certified (in countries with certification schemes)?
- (vi) Does it maintain and regularly update a detailed website?
- (vii) Does it publish independent evaluations of its activities?
- (viii) Is it transparent about its funding sources?
- (ix) Does it report decisions made by its governing board?
- (x)   Is it perceived as being reputable by the media, the public, or decision-makers?
- (xi) Does it insist on intellectual rigor and the use of facts in performing analyses?
- (xii) Does it adhere to agreements with other stakeholders?

What to look for: (i) a professional and informative website, (ii) favorable references in the media, (iii) listing in CSO directories, (iv) sincerity in engagement, (v) claims backed up by facts, (vi) actions consistent with stated mission, (vii) use by others as a source of reliable information, (viii) readiness to share information about its activities and the nature of the support it receives, and (ix) clarity about individuals' roles within the organization.

Mission and Governance

Questions:

    (i)   Does the CSO share ADB's overarching objective of poverty alleviation?

    (ii)   Does it have a long-term development vision?

(iii) Is it clear about its objectives and role?

(iv) Who are its staff and management officials?

(v)   Are there related individuals on the board?

(vi) Who serves on the governing body and what are the body's responsibilities?

(vii) How does the governing body exercise oversight?

(viii) Does it have a clearly communicated organizational structure?

What to look for: (i) coherent statement of mission, objectives, and vision; (ii) biographies of members of governing board and management; (iii) charter; and (iv) organizational chart.

Constituency and Support

Questions:

    (i)   Does the CSO have a clearly identified constituency?

    (ii)   Is the organization membership-based?

(iii) Does the CSO have regular, participatory links to its constituency?

(iv) Are constituents informed and supportive about the CSO and its activities?

(v)   Does the CSO belong to CSO thematic or sector associations, networks, or umbrella groups?

(vi) Does the CSO have strong links within the CSO community and to other social institutions?

(vii) Has the CSO conducted social audits (to assess its impact on society)?

(viii) Does the CSO have partnerships with other organizations engaged in development work (e.g., government agencies, international NGOs, foundations, UN agencies, other multilateral development banks)?

What to look for: (i) supportive statements from constituency members, (ii) activities geared to serve constituency, (iii) organizational affiliations, (iv) participation in conferences and workshops related to its primary field of activity, (v) partnerships with other reputable organizations, and (vi) record of sustained funding.

Technical Capacity

Questions:
Does the CSO

(i)   possess the required knowledge and technical skills?
(ii)   collect baseline information about its constituency?
(iii) keep informed about the latest techniques, competencies, policies, and trends in its area of expertise?
(iv)   apply effective approaches to reach its targets?
(v)   have a strong presence in the field?
(vi)   effectively coordinate between field and office?

What to look for: (i) tools, (ii) methodologies, (iii) evaluations, (iv) use of indicators and benchmarking, (v) databases, (vi) staff turnover, (vii) trained paid personnel and volunteers, and (viii) reports on technical experience from development agencies relating to operations and capacity building.

Managerial Capacity

Questions:
Does the CSO

(i)   produce clear, internally consistent proposals, and intervention frameworks?
(ii)   include a regular review in the development of a program, and organize program and project review meetings?
(iii) translate strategic planning into operational activities?
(iv)   monitor progress against indicators and evaluate achievements?
(v)   include the viewpoint of beneficiaries in the design and review of its programming?
(vi)   have clearly defined policies on gender equity, environmental sustainability, and human resource management?

What to look for: (i) well-designed project and program documents, (ii) evaluation and monitoring reports, and (iii) evaluations and impact studies.

Administrative Capacity

Questions:
Does the CSO

(i)   possess logistical infrastructure and equipment?
(ii)   manage and maintain equipment?
(iii) have the ability to produce goods, services, and works on a competitive basis?

What to look for: (i) adequate physical and logistical infrastructure, including office facilities, space, computers, and resource materials; (ii) standard contracts for procurement; and (iii) written procedures for identifying appropriate vendors (e.g., obtaining the best price, issuing commitments).

Financial Capacity

Q **Questions:**

Does the CSO

   (i) produce program and project budgets, and have a regular budget cycle?

   (ii) Aside from the budget, does the CSO prepare a financing strategy? A financing strategy is integral to an organization's strategic plan. This refers to the budget based on the organizational strategy and plan and how the CSO plans to finance its operations to meet its objectives and targets. In addition, does the CSO have a clear understanding of the values of the organization, values which cannot be compromised by the financing strategy?

   (iii) have a track record of managing large sums of money?

   (iv) ensure physical security of advances, cash, and records?

   (v) disburse funds in a timely and effective manner?

   (vi) have procedures relating to authority, responsibility, monitoring, and accountability of handling funds?

   (vii) boast a record of financial stability and reliability?

   (viii) keep well-organized, accurate, and informative accounts?

   (ix) ensure proper financial recording and reporting?

What to look for: (i) operating budgets and financial reports; (ii) list of donors and funding details; (iii) written procedures for accounts payable, receivables, stock, and inventory; (iv) a reporting system that tracks commitments and expenditures against budgets by line; (v) a bank account with regular statements; (vi) audited financial statements; (vii) a competent accounting system; and (viii) written procedures for processing payments and recording transactions.

Glossary

ADB-assisted project – A project financed or to be financed, or administered or to be administered, by ADB, and covers both sovereign and nonsovereign operations.

advocacy organization – An advocacy civil society organization engages in policy dialogue and other means to influence the views, policies, and actions of governments and other organizations and stakeholders, such as ADB, the media, and their community. This organization may also have an operational or service focus in addition to the advocacy focus, or may work exclusively as an advocacy organization.

affected people – Refers to the population receiving positive and/or negative impact of the intervention or project.

borrower – When applied to a sovereign operation, means the borrower of an ADB loan or the recipient of an ADB grant; and when applied to a nonsovereign operation, means the borrower, guarantee beneficiary, fund manager, investee, or similar entity to which ADB lends or guarantees, or in which it invests.

citizen – A member of a state; a native or naturalized person who owes allegiance to a government and is entitled to protection from it; a civilian as distinguished from a specialized servant of the state.[1]

civil society – The arena, outside of the family, the state, and the market which is created by individual and collective actions, organizations, and institutions to advance shared interests.[2]

civil society organization – Refers generically to organizations (i) not based in government, and (ii) not created to earn profit. ADB defines civil society organizations (CSOs) as nonprofit organizations independent from the government, which operate around common interests. They vary in size, interests, and function; and include nongovernment organizations (NGOs), youth groups, community-based organizations, independent academic and research institutes, professional associations, foundations, faith-based organizations, people's organizations, and labor unions. CSOs represent interests of their members or others.

corporate results framework – The ADB corporate results framework is a management tool that helps ADB monitor and improve its performance to achieve the goals set out in Strategy 2030.[3]

---

[1] Definition from Merriam-Webster Dictionary.
[2] CIVICUS. CIVICUS Enabling Environment.
[3] Asian Development Bank. ADB Results Framework.

nongovernment organization – A nonprofit organization, independent of government, that provides or advocates the provision of services relating to economic and social development, human rights, public welfare, or emergency relief.

operations department – Any department that handles the formulation, processing, or implementation of an ADB-assisted project. The operations departments include the regional departments and the Private Sector Operations Department.

policy – A statement of objectives or goals of ADB in a particular area of activity over a medium- to long-term period. Policy may also establish boundaries within which the management must choose its strategy and activities in pursuit of these objectives. Policy is a higher level of direction than strategy and other directional documents in the particular area of activity. Policy is more stable and interpreted more rigidly. Strategy is adjusted more frequently and applied more flexibly.

poor people – ADB's corporate results framework indicator definition is: "poor people" are those from households living on less than $1.90 a day.[4] This is based on the World Bank Group's International Poverty Line.[5] ADB also uses national and subregional poverty lines.

strategy – A set of options or means to achieve the objectives or goals established by a policy and/or the ADB Charter.

umbrella, peak, or apex civil society organization – A CSO that represents a group of CSOs either as a membership-based organization (with CSOs as members) or as coalitions, alliances, or networks, which are united by a common geography and/or membership or set of objectives or area of activity.

vulnerable people – Refer to (as relevant for a particular project) ethnic minorities, hard-to-reach remote populations, migrants, and internally displaced and/or conflict-affected people, persons with disability, returning refugees, HIV/AIDS-affected individuals and households, older persons, and households headed by women.[6]

Youth for Asia – ADB's Youth for Asia initiative enables youth and governments to work for a prosperous, inclusive, resilient, and sustainable Asia and the Pacific. Youth for Asia is youth-led and aims to mainstream meaningful youth engagement in ADB operations. The impact it seeks is for young citizens from across Asia and the Pacific to be engaged as partners to achieve inclusive and sustainable development results.

---

[4]   ADB. 2021. *Results Framework Indicator Definitions*. Manila.
[5]   World Bank. The International Poverty Line.
[6]   Footnote 4.

www.ingramcontent.com/pod-product-compliance
Lightning Source LLC
Chambersburg PA
CBHW050044220326
41599CB00045B/7274